The Dark Secrets of Woodruff County

KENT HANDY

AuthorsPress
California, USA
www.authorspress.com

Contents

This is a True Story

This is about five innocent kids who were murdered by race-haters and the alleged Ku Klux Klan in Woodruff County, Arkansas. Over the years, fourteen other black bodies have been found murdered by race-haters, and no one has spent a single night in jail for any of it.

If I had a dollar for every time that I wanted to write this book then I could have retired by now. Over the years, I have had all kinds of people telling me that they were going to help me write this book but didn't, so at the end of the day, I found myself by myself. And yet the story must be told, at least that is what I believe.

I wrote this book in honor of my family. To the five children who lost their lives at the hands of some race-haters, including the alleged Ku Klux Klan. To my grandmother Isdee Valentine and to my grandfather Shawnee Valentine (who passed away before I finished this book). To my aunt Nellie who lost her only son. I would like to give a special thanks to Mr. Wendell Teal for being a wonderful mentor. To my own dear mother, Mrs. Paula Jean Armstrong, whom I have found to be one of the strongest black woman I have ever known. To each and every family member who has gone through any difficult experience in this lifetime. Lastly, I would also like to dedicate this book to my wife and kids, for their patience, understanding, support, and love. Above all, I would like to thank God for having his hand in my life.

So please allow me to take you on a journey that could be described as a complicated yet highly appreciated life. My name is Kent Lemont

1

Handy, and I was born to Mr. William Handy and Ms. May West Valentine on October 22, 1960, in Little Rock, Arkansas. My mother would later change her name to what everybody had come to know her by—Paula Jean Armstrong. I am the second oldest child out of twelve children, and the only child that my mother had by my father. Most of the names of the characters have been changed to protect my family and myself. However, the names that you are about to read of my family are real.

Family

Coming up in the south in those days, almost everybody had a nickname. Part of the Southern culture is embracing nicknames given to you by family members and friends. For instance, my name is Kent, but my grandfather nicknamed me Kellogg, and sometimes my family would call me Dob Milan. Dob Milan was the man who used to babysit me along with his wife while my mother worked. The oldest child from my mother was named Joseph, but his nickname was Bishop. Being recently married to Curtis Armstrong, Warnell was the first child to be born to that union whose nickname was Roy. When Mama would leave, she would put me in charge and then she would lay down her rules of things to do and have done by the time that she got back and things what not to do. But as soon as Mama would leave, Warnell would make it his business to do the thing that Mama said don't do, so he and I would sometimes fight because I knew that as soon as Mama got back, I was going to be the one to get a whipping simply because I was who she left in charge. Then there was Gina, whose nickname was Bull, but she would later be called Arthur Jones after a man who later came into my mother's life; she never managed to get rid of her nickname. Then there was Vanessa, whose nickname was Collier. Then there was Dwayne who was known as Pressure. He got his hands on a retired judge's law books, and studied them, so whenever someone in the family had a question about the law, they would ask Dwayne. There was Shelia, who was called Tom. Unlike most other Southerners, there was Tracy who didn't have a nickname. There was Ryan who was called Tag, and Little Curtis who was called Booly. Kizzie, who was called Roe, was named after the lady that played the character Kizzie in Alex Haley's movie *Roots*. Little did she know, this nickname would one day carry a symbolic meaning and play an important role in her life. Finally, there was Bryan who occasionally was called Eddie Giddy, simply because he looked so much like his father Eddie. Eddie was the last man to come into my mother's life; he also was the father of Kizzie.

While these nicknames might fool you to think we just didn't bother to learn each other's names, we sincerely loved each other. My brother, Ryan, used to tell me that his nose looked similar to mine. Yet, like most sisters and brothers of larger family, we've had our share of disagreements as well. We would argue over the little things like "who told you to put on my shoes or shirt without asking me?" Then there were times when we shared our deepest fears and secrets. Ryan used to come home and tell me how scared he was of a man from Augusta born with polio. He told me the man walked with a limp, and one of his arms was shorter than the other. One day, Warnell held Ryan and told the man to come and touch Ryan with his shortest arm. When the man walked over to Ryan, I saw my brother's eyes filled up with fear. I could tell his heart was galloping faster than a racehorse.

Ryan became so afraid that he fainted.

Little Curtis was quiet and shy. Tracy was somewhat quiet and mild-tempered, but you would miss her when she was not around. Bryan was one of those kids who was seven going on seventeen. He was what the old folks down south used to call "too smart for his age." When I, or anyone else, talked with Bryan, you could easily forget that he was only seven years old. And because we were such a large family, sometimes we would hang out in pairs. There was Shelia and Tracy, Gina and Vanessa, Ryan and Curtis, and because I was the second oldest, I could hang out with Joe, who was the oldest, or Warnell, who was younger. But no matter what age group you fell in, Mama made sure that we all knew that we were a family.

From the time that I was between the age of one and five years old, I lived with Mr. Dob Milan and his wife Mrs. Dmitry Milan.

My mother was working as a nurse, and because she worked all the time, she didn't have a lot of time to spend with me. She would come and see me and bring me things, but I thought that Mr. Dob and his wife were my parents because they had a direct role in my upbringing as a child. Dob worked as a lumberjack, and his wife stayed at home with me. Sometimes he let me ride with him in his work truck. The ride was usually loud from the truck especially when he changed the gears and clutched. Some nights, I would sleep right between the two of them. I remember using Dob's arm as a pillow. One night while I was sleeping with them, I had a dream that I had a cake, and I wanted some of it, but they wouldn't not give me a piece, so I woke up in the middle of the night whining, saying, "Give me my cake," and they responded, "What cake? You don't have a cake, so go back to sleep." But I kept crying until I got a spanking and came back to reality and realized that it was only a dream. Dob took me to a bar once, and he put me on a stage and asked me to dance. People were throwing money at me. Then someone came up to Dob and said, "The boy's mother is outside." Once I heard the person's remark, I jumped down off the stage and ran out of the bar onto the sidewalk. I saw my mother running toward me, I remember her hair bouncing as she was running to pick me up to hug and kiss me full of excitement. Needless to say, I missed my mother.

After I got the chance to visit my mom, I went back home with Dob, but it wasn't too long after that, when one day, my mother and her uncle who was named Uncle Golden, who lived in Kansas City, Missouri, came to Dob's house to pick me up.

Only this time, it was for good. My mother had decided to move back from Little Rock to the little small town where her parents lived in—Woodruff County. Dob and his wife were begging my mother not to take me. They began to cry as my mother tried to take me away. In my head, I was already home, I didn't need to be anywhere else. Plus, my father William Handy Sr. and my grandmother Mrs. Evil Handy lived just across town. I didn't want to get in the car, but Uncle Golden spanked me and put me in the car. That was the beginning of a whole new life.

Home to Home

Years later, I realized that the Milans had gotten attached to me as if I were their own true biological son. The fact that they couldn't have children of their own didn't help either. However, my mother was only paying them as my babysitter. It was never her intention to give me away. Yet, I was only five years old at the time, and I was feeling like I had been taken from my parents and home.

Around dusk dark, we arrived in Augusta, Woodruff County. I found myself around a lot of people that I didn't know. I noticed that everyone seemed to be very excited to see me. It seemed like forever since I had seen my family. It felt as though I was seeing them all for the first time. My last memories of them didn't seem to match my reality. They had matured and aged with my time away. My mother had quit her job in Little Rock in order to relocate to a small town that would fit her small budget. During this time, I witnessed my mother struggle to maintain a comfortable life for herself and her children. She planned to depend on some of her family members to lend her a helping hand. Yet the problem was they didn't have much for themselves. I can remember playing outside one day when I found a twenty- dollar bill, and one of my uncles saw me when I picked it up, then he started running after me so he could take it. I wanted that twenty-dollar bill so I sprinted faster and eventually made it to my mother to give it to her. I knew she didn't have any money. As a child from poverty, I understand that when you're dead broke, twenty dollars seem like all the riches in world, especially back in that day when twenty dollars got you a lot. Times were hard.

My mother eventually decided to leave our small town and move back to the city. But this time, it wasn't going to be Little Rock. She wanted to move to an area that provided as much opportunity as possible so she could provide a stable home for her children. That place was the big city of Chicago. Yet once again, she reached out to her family to ask them to look after us while she moved to Chicago to find a job and home for all of us. Being that our family is so big, she already knew she would have a place to stay.

Meanwhile, we were going from one relative to another. Eventually, I ended up staying with my aunt Janie (my mother's sister), her husband, and children. Her husband, Uncle Johnny (Johnny Rat), was a farmer and worked on what was known at that time as the Cesar farm. Surprisingly enough, it was kind of cool to live on the farm. It wasn't much to do, but we made the best of it. They owned a goat and named it Bomb, and we would ride it sometimes. We even took a can of white spray paint and painted the numbers sixty-six on its side. Now, the Cesars were so powerful and rich that the little town of Gregory was named in their honor. Uncle Johnny had worked for the Cesars all of his life; he had worked his way up to be the head farmer. And he had credit at what was known as the Gregory store, and it was owned by the Cesars as well. And by taking on the responsibility to feed extra mouths, he had to use his credit quite often.

During my time there, I experienced some new things. For one, it was the first time that I ever heard the word welfare and commodity. Although blacks were not getting welfare because the whites didn't tell them about it—or that it even existed. But blacks were getting the commodity, which consisted of pork in a can, chicken in a can, a box of cheese, and a box of raisins. And let me tell you that they were glad to get that. A black man would be responsible for delivery of the commodity to the blacks especially to those that lived in the country. The commodity truck only ran once a month, but there was another truck that ran each month, and it was a white man driving it. It was a sweet ride because it was a candy truck. It amazes me when I go into a store today and see some of that same kind of candy that I used to see on that candy truck when I was just a little boy. Like the three- colored coconut bar, the peanut roll, and the yellow-and-white corn candy to name a few. This was a special time in my life.

During this time, I met my great-grandmother, Nellie McKnight, for the first time. Everybody called her Mama Nellie. At the time, she lived with her daughter, and they had just moved back to Arkansas from California. My great-aunt had ten children and raised them all by herself because their father stayed in California. She had little help raising her children. Her main source of assistance came from her elderly mom and dad, when they could. And I will be the first to say that she did a very fine job raising her children despite the little help she got from her family. They lived deep in the woods, and you know that nobody can watch ten kids at the same time. They were bad, and I mean bad. They were the original "bebe kids," so we used to call them savages. Let's use your imagination just for a little while, imagine you are walking down a narrow dirt road that's deep in the woods.

It is very quiet, and the only sound that you hear is the yapping of some birds and you are saying to yourself just how peaceful and beautiful it is back here. Then unexpectedly your concentration is broken by someone jumping from behind a tree to slap you in the back of the head and then run their hand down from your forehead across your lips. All at the same time yelling out a word that you don't even understand. But from what you could make out, it sounds something like "Lea tee!" Just as fast as they came out of those woods, they would be gone back into them. May be now you can see why we were calling them savages.

On the weekends, Uncle Johnny would take us to the little farm store where he had credit. It was also the place where he would pick up his paycheck; they would cash it for him and then take out the money for the things that he had already credited. Then with what he had left, he would buy things like a pack of cigarettes or bullets for his gun because he loved to hunt.

Occasionally, he would buy himself a new pair of work boots and so forth. In other words, the farm would pay him and then turn right around and get most of it back. It kept him in a position where he would always need more credit. By the time he got through buying us kids candy, such as pops and honey buns, he wouldn't have much left for himself. He would then take us back home, but he would then head off to town, Augusta, Arkansas, to hang out with the fellows. Augusta is like the headquarters in Woodruff County, also known as the County Seat. Augusta was located eleven miles north of Gregory.

Uncle Johnny had an old car but it didn't work, so he had to catch a ride or, in those days, hitchhike a ride to and from town. Also in those days, in the south, if you had a car that didn't work, people would just push it into the backyard, or in many cases, they would just use them for storage. Yet, even to this day, you can ride through some of the small towns in Arkansas and see some old trucks and cars in backyards. Because they don't use salt in the winter, like most states up north, those old cars and trucks can last in those backyards for years. Uncle Johnny's house set out in the open, but only a few yards away on the east side of their house was the woods, which was sometimes called the thickest, wood line, and sometimes a fencerow. It was where the land stop and the woods began. The house was about a half a mile off of the main highway that ran between Augusta and Gregory on a road that has never been paved. Most people down south would call it a gravel road. Anyway, instead of them pushing his old car to the backyard, they pushed it into the woods. After a couple of years had gone by, one day, we adventured into the woods by that old car. And we noticed a buzzing sound coming from the car, so we began to investigate, only to discover that the car had set up for such a long time, some honeybees had made a honeycomb full of honey in the backseat. So we simply eased away from the car, but a few days later, we decided to get the honey. It was good and sweet, and with all the mouths to feed, we surely could use it. Not knowing any better, we started to throw dirtballs at the bees trying to run them off so that we could get the honey. But we soon learned that all we had done was to stir them up and got one of the young men that were with us stung.

When Uncle Johnny came home and heard about what happened with the young man getting stung, he began to tell us what we had done wrong: "First of all, you can't use dirt to run off the bees."

Then he began to tell us the right way to get the honey, "All you have to do is find some old clothes and set them on fire then put them out and let them smoke. Once the bees smell the smoke, they would leave for safety thinking that the woods were on fire. Then you can walk up and get the honey." It all made sense to me.

He also indicated that the dirt would have only ruin the honey. So we took his advice and to our amazement, it worked. Sometimes it would be late when Uncle Johnny got a ride back home from town. But no matter how late it would be when he got back, he would still get up early in the morning and go to work on time. You could hear him rattling his pots and dishes as he makes him a cup of Maxwell House coffee. The next thing that you would hear would be the front door opening, and the last thing that you would hear was the slamming of the screen door. But the sweet aroma of the coffee would linger on in the house. Many times I have looked out of the window at him as he would be walking down to the farm shop where he worked if they were not drivinga tractor in the fields.

My mother had found Chicago to be too big and too fast for her, and she definitely was not trying to raise her children there. So she moved back to Augusta, Woodruff County, and got us, and moved us a few miles just south of Gregory to a little town called Little Dixie. We moved into a small house that only had about three rooms. With a small front yard that set just a few feet off the same main highway that my grandparents and Uncle Johnny lived. But right off the backyard was a grain bin. This was during the time when Arthur Jones was living with us, the man Gina received her nickname from. Arthur and I looked in that grain bin and it was a wild rabbit in there that Arthur killed with his feet. I guess you know that later on that day we had fried rabbit.

Now, Little Dixie was located between Gregory and Cotton Plant, Arkansas, which was still Woodruff County. And one day, my mother went off for a while, and she left my oldest brother, Joe, in charge. But as soon as Mom left, Joe talked me into walking to our grandparents' house that was about eleven miles away. Joe was only about twelve years old, and I was only about seven years old. It was daytime when we first started walking, but it got night on us, and it seem like we were never going to get there. It was a very dangerous thing to do, to be walking in Woodruff County, young and black, at night from Little Dixie to Gregory was almost suicide. It was summertime in Woodruff County, and if the Ku Klux Klan didn't get you then the mosquitoes surely would. I was wearing short pants, and I had never walked that long or that far before in my entire seven years. My grandparents' house set high off the ground, and after we got there, Joe wanted to play with them by crawling up under the house to make some noise and try to scare them but I was tired. Plus, the mosquitoes had just about eaten me alive; I wanted to just go inside the house. After all, we were so young and lived so faraway; we would have been the last persons that they would have expected to see after dark and especially under their house. It doesn't take a rocket scientist to figure out what happened to us for leaving home without permission. And let me tell you back then those old houses were just that, old. Back in that day, it was not uncommon to walk in a black person's home, and see a barrel or a tin can with their flour, meal, and crackers in it. But in my grandparents' case, it would be an old wooden trunk to keep out the mice. They had a hogpen on the side of the house toward the back. And every now and then, a hog would get out and head straight for the side door in that bedroom where that old wooden trunk would be. If it was left unlocked the hogs would get into it. But if it was locked all the hogs could do was push it around.

♦

Injustice

It wasn't too long before my mom was moving back to Chicago. This meant that Joe and I would be moving, once again, with our grandparents. With eight of their eleven children still living at home, it could easily be as many as four people to one bed. And because my grandmother was only fifteen when she married, my mother started having children before my grandmother stopped. So that made me and some of my uncles close to the same age, and I am older than some of my aunts. So I mostly interacted with the youngest kids, which would have been my uncle Alvin and aunt Darleen and aunt Earlean which were twins. My aunt Lula was the youngest.

I started school out of my grandparents' house. And my grandfather worked as a bus driver, but not just a bus driver—my bus driver. Every morning, our day would start with the same routine. Grandpa would make a cup of coffee, but he would never drink all of it. Instead, he would leave a little in the cup just for me to finish it. Then he would say, "All right, let's go!" Lula would then start crying because she didn't want to go to school, she just wanted to stay at home with Grandma. Every morning was like clockwork. When Grandpa would say, "All right let's go!" you could look forward for Lula to start crying. She would start in the house but wouldn't stop until she was on the bus, and that would be only after Grandpa had made a stop or two picking up other schoolkids.

Now, I am in school for the first time in my life. I am only seven years old, and one morning, as I enter into the building right in the middle of the hallway, I see a group of young boys gathering around. So I go closer to see what all of the commotion is about. I notice that one of the boys has another boy in a headlock. When I got closer, I realized that all the other boys that had gathered around to kick the distressed boy as they passed by, so as I passed by I kicked him too. As time went by, I later learned their names, it was Cavan Smith that had Willie Frank in the headlock. Our determined fate would allow us all to become the best of friends. I had started to look forward to going to school every day, but my aunt Lula was still crying every morning. Then to everyone's surprise, one morning when Grandpa said, "All right, let's go!" Lula didn't cry. She had accepted the fact that she had to go to school like the rest of us.

At seven years of age, I didn't have the opportunity to use computers or play all of the games that kids have today, so we had to make up games. Darleen, Earlean, and I made up this game called "Doo Dee Gail" who was a make-believe ghost. And some nights we would go to bed, but not to sleep. Instead, we would be up talking and the older kids knew that we were afraid of Doo Dee Gail. So they would yell "here comes Doo Dee Gail," turn off the lights, and shut the door. We would put our little heads under the cover and would be almost too afraid to breathe, thinking that Doo Dee Gail would hear us, and come and get us. They were very supposition in those days, and say stuff like "don't split the pole, if a black cat crosses the street to your left then it's bad luck but if it crosses to your right then it's good luck. And if you're left eye jumped, it was bad luck but if your right eye jumped then it was good luck."

Another thing that they were very supposition about would be that on New Year's Day. You couldn't sweep trash out after dark because if you did, they believe that your house would burn down, you also couldn't wash, iron, or sew on New Year's Day. And the first person to enter the house on New Year's Day that didn't live there had to be a man for good luck. If someone opened the door to let a woman in first, it was bad luck for the house, and by the time they finish beating you, it was bad luck for you too. Also, you had to cook and eat black-eyed peas on New Year's Day for good luck.

I had what the old folks down south call a good grade of hair. Darleen and Earlean both love to comb my hair. Darleen would be on one side of my head, and Earlean would be on the other, and because of my family's supposition, they would say that it was bad luck for two people to be on a head at the same time, because the youngest one would die. But they didn't believe that stuff, so the both would keep combing my hair.

One spring-like day, while I was living at my grandparents, it rained heavily. So much it filled the big ditch that was in front of the house and then it stopped. So my uncles, siblings, and the rest of the family started swimming in the big ditch. We were wrestling, playing, and having so much fun. Then it started to rain again so my aunt Nellie made us get out of the ditch and come in the house and out of the rain. And so we did, we were watching television but eventually I had to use the bathroom, so I got up and started through the back of the house where the bathroom was. But on my way, I noticed that the side door that the hogs would come in was open, and when I looked out of it, I noticed the rain stopped. So I thought that it must be all right to go back outside to play in the water, and so I did. I came out of that side door and walked from the back of the house to the front yard, and then I crossed the street to get a running start to jump in the big ditch that was filled with rainwater. But before I could start my run, I noticed Earlean had come out of that same door, and she was walking toward me. She was smiling as she began to cross and come to where I was. I looked both ways down the highway, and I saw this car coming from Gregory's way and it was coming fast heading toward Augusta, so I yelled out to Earlean, "Go back, it's coming too fast!" She went back and walked on the edge of the highway, off of the black top, and on the gravel waiting for the oncoming car to pass. Then all of a sudden, the next thing I heard was the sound of tires swerving and the loud sound of something being hit. I was too small to look over the top of the car to see if Earleen was still on the side of the highway because the car had come to a stop between her and me. About that time, everybody was coming out of the house, and it only took a second for them to realize what had just happened. Then all I could hear was screaming, yelling, and crying. I had to cross back over the highway and go around the car to see what everybody was screaming about. But as I crossed back over the highway, I noticed that the driver of the car, which was a white man, was trading places with the passenger of the car which was a white woman. I didn't understand why they were doing that at that time because I was only seven years old. Then I saw everyone gathering at the back of the school bus that my grandfather drove. So I walked over toward them as I made my way through the crowd I see her. I could see the white of Earleen's eyes as they roll back in her head. There was gravel in her hair, and one of her legs was bigger than the other. It looked like that car had knocked her at least fifty feet from where I last saw her walking. Someone said that it was my fault, and that if I had just stayed in the house that she might not have come outside. I don't know if we can miss death or not, but I do know that there are things that we can do to prevent it, unless it is just our time to go. Either way, I wish that I would have stayed in that house. Since we lived eleven miles from Augusta, it seem like it took forever for an ambulance to get there. Earleen died before she got to the hospital or shortly after, and just like that, my little aunt was gone. We later found out that the people in that car had stopped at a service station about a mile and a half before they got to us to buy gas, and in those days, the service station attendant would clean your windshield and check all of your fluids. The station owner told them that they had bad brakes, but when they paid for gas, he could smell alcohol on their breaths. Yes, you have heard me right, Earleen had been killed by a drunk driver. Who didn't get charged with anything. No jail, no court, and as far as I am concerned, no justice. The man later gave my grandparents three thousand dollars along with an "I'm sorry for your daughter's precious life."

Now let us put the shoe on the other foot for just a little while. What do you think the outcome would have been if the driver of that car would have been a black man and the little girl that he hit and killed was white? With the owner of the service station saying that he had warn them about their brakes and that he smelled alcohol on their breath. Well, let me help show you the answer to that, do you remember a few years ago? A case that was in the news about a little black boy who was only six years old at the time, how he had taken a gun to school and shot and killed his little classmate who just happens to be a little white girl, and because the child was too young to be prosecuted then the authorities went after the little six-year-old black boy's parents. It was as if the authorities had said in their heart that somebody is going to pay for killing this little white girl. Now please don't get me wrong because I don't, in anyway, want you to misunderstand me. My heart goes out to that little girl, and I don't care what color she was. My heart also goes out to her family, I am so sorry for their lost. But why would the authorities go after the parents of the little black child as if they told him to do that. When in reality it was a terrible mistake. I mean, the key word here is "mistake." It just seems to me that the authorities would understand that the parents of the young black child already had to live with the fact that their child had taken a life. And being that young, the chances are the child doesn't really know what he has done.

In Colorado, there were a couple of guys, not six year olds, but teenagers, who happened to be white and were still living at home with their parents. They had taken guns to school and intentionally shot and killed more than one person. No one went to the killers' house to arrest their parents nor did the authorities go to the parents of those in Jonesboro, Arkansas. So what's wrong with this picture? All that I am really trying to say is that the law is the law and no one should be above it—black or white.

When Earleen died that day, it was a long and sad day. Can you imagine what it must to have been like for me being only seven years old and being told that the reason that Earleen was dead and the reason that everybody was crying was because of me? And can you imagine what it must to have been like for Darleen and I to go to bed that night without Earleen?

It was a very long night, and we had so many mixed feelings, we were already afraid of Doo Dee Gail. We wanted Earleen to be home, but at the same time, we were afraid to see her ghost, because we knew that she was dead. My grandparents didn't want to live in that house anymore so they moved to town. The same town that my Uncle Johnny used to catch a ride to and from. Yap, you guessed it right, it was Augusta. When the news of Earleen's death reached Chicago, my mother and her brothers came home to bury their little seven-year-old sister. And shortly after that, my stepfather came home from prison. So my mother didn't go back to Chicago. Instead, he moved us; meaning my mother,

Warnell, Gina, Vanessa, Dwayne, and myself; with Dwayne being the youngest at that time because Shelia and the rest of the kids had not been born yet. But Joe stayed with our grandparents while the rest of us moved to a small town in Woodruff County called Cotton Plant. As you can see, it was already hard times growing up in Arkansas with it being the second poorest state in the union, with only Mississippi being number one.

To be black, poor, and to live in a time when there was no cell phones, no microwaves, no video games. If you were blessed enough to personally own a television set, it was most likely shown in black and white. Ours didn't have a knob so we had to use a pair of pliers to change the channel. There was no such thing as cable television, you would have to use a tall antenna, and you would need two people to work it. One on the outside turning it while the other person is in the house watching for a clear picture as he or she be yelling through the wall to tell the other one that's turning it to stop when he gets a clear signal.

Television would sign off the air every night at midnight to live in a time period such as that was an incredible experience.

Daddy, who I had come to know as my stepfather, had explained to us that a man named Mr. Gino Green had come to the prison and got him out on a work program. If you were white and owned a farm in those days in Arkansas, you could do that. There were not many blacks that owned their own farm, maybe some small piece of ground that they would call a farm. But if they would have gone to a prison and ask for a white man to work for them, they would have most likely been denied. We, as kids, were very glad about it, we could see that our mother was happier, and we were finally settled in our own house and not staying with this and that relative. But be it to our surprise after a while, Daddy was not happy. He was put in a bad position. He wanted to be home with his family like any normal man would. Daddy thought that Mr. Gino Green was taking advantage of his situation. By working him from sunup to sundown, Daddy used to say that he didn't work that hard in prison. It was either do it or he would send him back to prison. Although Daddy was not happy with the treatment that he was receiving from Mr. Green, he never wanted to go back to prison. He would often say that if he knew today he was going to go back to prison tomorrow that he would've just killed himself. I used to hate to hear him say that, simply because I loved him.

Another reason why Daddy was so unhappy was because Mr. Green had brought Daddy a car, a little Chevy II, and he told Daddy that he had paid twelve hundred dollars for it and that he could pay him back by allowing him to take money out of his check every week. About three years later, he was still taking money out of daddy's check for that car. Daddy thought that he had already paid him back for that car and some, he felt that it was just another form of slavery, you know "as long as you owe me, you can't leave me" kind of thing. But to tell you the truth I kind of liked Cotton Plant. For once, everybody except Joe was under one roof.

Nostalgia

I was in a new school, and I had made some new friends. I even had a little crush on my teacher's daughter, and her daddy was the principal at that time, but years later, he became the school's superintendent. I used to love the smell of fresh air in the country, and you could smell the rain afar off. The closest house was about a block away, so we had lots of space to run and play without disturbing our neighbors. Who on one side was Mr. Stanley and Jean Rice, and on the other side was a man called Mr. J. W. Tail. Warnell and I would venture down to the cash river to see the turtles on the logs as they would bathe in the sun. Also, there was a large pile of sawdust that had some small lizards living in there, and we would try to catch them, but most of the time their tails would break off. The tails would still be moving, but the lizard would have gotten away. Mr. Green had some farm animals, he had cows, bulls, two big dogs; and he would buy some wild horses for Daddy to ride and break, by riding it in a muddy field until it was tired out to take the fight out of it. Mr. Green had two humpback bulls; one was named Big John and the other one was called Wood Da Maker. The two dogs were Great Danes, and their names were Happy and Hobo.

One day, Warnell and I went walking down to the shop to see the cows and to see what kind of work that Daddy was doing. But Hobo and Happy ran out to meet us, they just wanted to play, but we didn't really know them plus they looked so big until we turned and ran for the house. They chased us all the way back; it was a while before we got the nerves to touch them. I can still remember the walks that we used to take on those warm summer nights under the light of a full moon, down that little dirt road barefooted, with the cool dust coming up between our toes. One night, while we were on a walk, out of the fog came two big objects. It's Big John and Wood Da Maker on a night stroll. Our walk was cut short that night because we broke for the house. Daddy brought some hogs to raise he had said that he was going to kill and eat one day. But we, as kids, had gotten attached to them and had given them names. We named the white male Earl, the black-and-white male Bow, and the female Lady. Now, Lady was very small, she was what they call the runt of the litter. She was just as old as the others, but Lady act more like a dog than a hog. I say that because she would come in the house, and if we were taking a nap, she would get in the bed with us and nap right along with us. Lady was very intelligent, she would walk to the bus stop with us which was about three blocks from the house, and sometimes she would be there in the evening waiting to walk us home.

Daddy traded the Chevy for a Dodge Charger with a fastback, this allowed us to go to Augusta on weekends. It was a late night when we would leave to go back home to Cotton Plant. I can remember lying in the back of the Charger looking out of the window of the fastback at the stars. Now that we had a new car, either we were going to Augusta or they were coming to Cotton Plant. Finally, Daddy decided to move to Augusta, and it won't be anymore late-night trips from Augusta back to Cotton Plant. But Mr. Green was trying to keep Daddy on his farm by asking my mother to try to talk Daddy into staying. He even started letting me ride a horse, and he was telling me that if we stayed I could ride it whenever I wanted to. But Daddy was not trying to hear that. He had made up his mind to leave Cotton Plant and move to Augusta, but there was one small problem: Daddy said that we cannot take the hogs with us, and that he was going to take them to the slaughterhouse. Us kids begged him not to.

He mercifully decided that he would kill one of them and give the rest of them away. We begged him not to kill Lady, so Earl was chosen to die. At first, Daddy had the gun aiming at Earl's head trying to get a good shot, but it was as if Earl knew that something was wrong. Earl would look up at Daddy and then put his head right back down so

Daddy couldn't get a good shot. Eventually, Daddy said that he could not do it. I was on pins and needles and just as I got a glimpse of hope that Earl was going to live, one of the other men who was standing around watching asked Daddy to give the gun to him and he would do it, so Daddy did. The man took aim and then he pull the trigger, blood splattered, and Earl was dead. Then the man ran up to Earl and took his knife and cut his throat so that he could bleed out quick. I can still remember the smell of Earl's hot fresh blood. I watched Earl get killed, and there was nothing that I could do about it. To them, they were just killing a hog; but to us, kids, they were killing our pet. So as you can see, Cotton Plant has played a very important part of my life.

The small town has set aside a day to honor itself, it is called Cotton Plant Day, and although many of the people have moved away to different cities all across the United States, many of them come back each year for that one special day. I have often wondered whatever happened to Lady and Bow. I also realized that Hobo, Happy, Big John, and Wood Da Maker are all gone now, but there is still one thing that remains until this day, and that is a big-time feast in a small-time town—Cotton Plant Day. On October 22, 1970, we moved from Cotton Plant to Augusta; it was on my tenth birthday. We moved in a house that sits on a land that was next door to the Woodruff County shop. Although I really didn't want to leave Cotton Plant, I was glad to be in Augusta, because now I was close to my grandparents and my uncles and aunts. Plus my aunt that used to live in the back of the woods with the bebe kids, well, they had moved to Augusta also.

It was all of us in one small town, and it was time to find out just who was who. So I learn that if I wanted to just take it easy then I needed to hang out with my uncles, but if I wanted the action then I needed to run with my cousins, the bebe kids.

Because that's where the action was; the older I got, the more we hung out. They loved the great outdoors and so did I. We would go fishing and bike riding. Once we rode our bikes all the way from Augusta to Gregory and back, oh boy, did they get me in trouble. I would stay all night without asking my mom, knowing that I was going to get a whipping. Daddy had landed a good job at what was known at that time as the Augusta Cooperation. And he did not want me to hang out with my cousins, because they would stay out late sometime, and I would hang right with them knowing that I was going to be in trouble. I had gotten to know a lot of people, and they had gotten to know me. We even put up a basketball net. I was pretty good at it, and I had made a little name for myself.

Augusta was a small town that seems to have stood still with time. It had a population sign that read: Three Thousand Six Hundred and Twenty-Four. For the longest time, no matter how long a person would leave and come back, the population sign would still say the same, and the town would still look the same.

About half of the population was black, and most of which was poor. With only a few of them making a good living, it was a small divided town. Yet those that we thought were making a good living or those that we perceived to have been rich lived on the north end of town. But the poor and those that we had perceived to be the middle class lived on the south end of town. So in order for us, meaning my cousins and me, to get some money, we would go up to the north end, and knock on the rich white folks' doors and ask for work. We would get little odds and ins jobs, like cutting grass, raking leaves, cleaning flower bed, and washing windows just to name a few. Compared to Little Dixie and Cotton Plant, Augusta was a fast town. Some of the blacks had either been to or lived in some of the big cities all across the United States. And because Augusta was the county seat, people was always coming and going to and from Augusta from the surrounding towns in Woodruff County. It was not a lot of black-on-black killings in those days. I can only remember one killing; that was when two black men were arguing, one went to his car to the trunk, and the other one thought that he was getting a gun, so he shot him in the back. Other than that about the only excitement you would get around there was, and if there was, a house fire. During those days there were only about four bars and grills in Augusta, two for the white folks and two for the black folks. Now, one of the bars for the white folks was located right in the heart of town, but the other one was all the way on the north end of town on the main highway that passed through the town which was US Route 64. But the blacks' bars were located about middle ways of town but on the edge of town. One of the bars for the blacks was named Jerry's, and the other one was called May Hearts. Now, May Hearts was a place for the old folks, but Jerry's was mostly for the young people, and that's where my cousins would hang out at. Like I said earlier, if I wanted action, I had to hang with the *bebe* kids.

There I was, only about fifteen years old, and I am out at the café trying to hang out. When I close my eyes, I can still hear the voices of all of those folks as they would all be trying to talk altogether with a little laughter. The room would be filled with cigarette smoke; you could see the thickness of it from the light that hung down over the pool table. I remember a little old lady that was cooking and selling sandwiches, while others would be on the dance floor, dancing and slow dancing, as some set at the bar ordering drinks and sandwiches. I had never seen anything like that before. I mean the way that men and women were holding each other as they were slow dancing I could only wonder what that felt like. I was growing up and it felt good, but one night as I was out in the café, my daddy stepped through the door and out of all of the noise that was in that places, it seem like everybody stopped just to hear what daddy was going to say to me. He called my name really loud and followed it with a "let's go home right now!" Needless to say, I was embarrassed.

It felt like every eyeball in the joint was upon me as I would exit the place. But it was too late, I had gotten a taste of what the nightlife of adults was like, so every now and then, I would sneak back out there again. Likewise, Daddy would either send someone in to tell me that he was outside, or he would come in and get me himself. Either way, he made sure to embarrass me, it took me a while but I finally got it.

I had come to realize that he did it all out of love. He simply didn't want me to grow up too fast. The white-folk bar that was in the heart of town didn't allow blacks to come in through the front door. They had to enter in through the rear entrance and remain in the back. They could not go up in the front of the building and socialize with the whites. There was only one hotel in Augusta, and it had the only public swimming pool in town. But blacks were not allowed to swim in it, so we would go to the White River to swim. It was fun but it was also very dangerous.

The water was swift with strong undercurrents and suckholes, but we had nowhere else to go so we risked it all. We would swim out to the steel barges that carried grain down to the mighty Mississippi, climb up on them, and dive off on the other side. And that would put us about middle ways of the White River. We would dive and swim so far down in the water until our ears would pop. And we would grab a handful of mud from the bottom to show everybody that you could hold your breath long enough to get to the bottom. But even though you could get a handful of mud, sometimes we would descend so far down in the water that by the time you would swim back up to the top to get air, your hand would not have any mud in it. And because the water ran all the time, the bottom of the river felt cold and slick. During the rainy season, the banks of the river would flood over into the fields, and when the waters would retread it would leave some fish trapped. So we would roll up our pants legs and go catch them with our bare hands, and most of the time, they would either be what they called German carp or buffalo fish, and then comes the fish fry.

We used to go in the empty new houses and play; turn on lights, run water, and make believe that it was our house. That is until people started to move in and eventually all of the houses were full, and there were no more empty houses to play in. Speaking of the projects, I was only around twelve years old when Daddy first started to talk about building and owning our own new home. I was feeling like a little man, the girls had started to look at me, and I was much more conscious about my appearance. We had a new four-bedroom brick home, even if it was a project. Life was looking up for us, Daddy had landed that good job, and I also had noticed that whenever we would be out in public, people would say, "Mr. Curtis this and Mr. Curtis that," so as you can see, we had respect from most of the black folks and from some of the white folks. Mr. Curtis Mayfield had came out with a song that said something like this, "You may not drive a great big Cadillac or even have a car at all, so just be thankful, brothers and sisters, for what you got 'cause you can still stand tall." Then the song went on to say, "Diamond in the back, sunroof top diggin' the scene with a gangsta lean, wooh-ooh-ooh... Gangsta whitewalls TV antennas in the back." So as the hood would have it, Daddy went out and bought a Cadillac. He had the top padded with the shape of a diamond in the back window, and the car was only two years old. It was almost a brand-new car. I shared that I was feeling like a man, and the truth be told I was acting like one too.

That's why Daddy was getting me out of the café, and sometimes Warnell and I would stay out a little late past suppertime. Mama would say, "Go eat your supper and go to bed," but Daddy didn't play that. He would say, "If you come in past supper then you go to bed hungry." So we would go to bed and wait until we thought that they had fallen asleep. We would get back up and raid the refrigerator. One night, we got caught by Daddy. He had laid waiting on us to try to steal food. So Warnell and I developed a system with codes so whenever we would come home past suppertime, we already knew that Daddy was expecting for us to just go on to bed so we would. But then we would get back up, but this time instead of rushing out of the room into the hallway and going straight to the refrigerator, we would go to the bathroom first. If by chance, Mom was up then we would say that it's the "city cop." If it was Daddy, we would say it's the state trooper. But if we didn't see either of them then we would say "the coast is clear."

One night, we were going to come out of the room then we heard something. Daddy knew that it was just a matter of time before we would be coming down that hallway trying to steal some late-night stacks. So to be on the safe side, Warnell put a hat on a broomstick. It was dark with all the lights off and stuck it out into the hallway, and Daddy raped it with a belt. He was waiting just outside our room in the hallway with all of the lights off. When he realized that it was just a hat and a broomstick he had whipped, he got mad but it was funny at the same time. We realized that it just wasn't worth the risk. Besides, late-night cold cuts could not match up to Mama's good hot home-cooked meals anyway. So we started to get home on time. There were no home computers, cell phones, iPads, Facebook, Instagram, or Twitter. Yet, we would still find ways to have some fun.

There were a few mom-and-pop stores around. At that time, food stamps came in little booklets, and it looked like play money. And when we would go to the small stores and buy something with the food stamps, instead of them giving us coin change back, they would write on a piece of paper how much they owe us, and they would call that piece of paper a due bill. In reality, they were making their own money and you couldn't spend it nowhere else but where you got it. I doubt if the federal government knew that was going on. We use to pick up and sell pop bottles to those small stores just to have money to buy candy. And there have been a few times that if the store stacked them up on the outside then we would steal them and take them to another store and sell them. We didn't mean any harm, we were just kids and it was just something to do in a small town.

Although we were not allowed to swim in the only swimming pool in town, many of the white kids still wanted to play with us. Some of the white kids' parents wouldn't allow it but little by little we interacted. It wasn't long before we were able to recognize the white folks that just didn't like blacks at all. Once you found out who they were then you would have little to no dealing with them. Sometimes your older family members would have told you who they knew was a member of the Ku Klux Klan. My mom told me once that when she was a young girl, she was at one of the little stores that were in Gregory. And at that time, this store was owned by a black man and was called Poor Boys so all the blacks would hang out there. But across the street was the little store that was owned by the Cesars, it was the same store that my uncle Johnny would take us to some years later. But at that time, the white folks use to hang out there. Mom said that one day, a black man walked across the street to ask those white men something, but a Klansman by the name of Whisper Dooley kicked the black man in the seat of his pants as he walked all the way back across the street. My mom said that he kicked him so hard until the black man's hat flew off his head. You had to learn how to survive, because their mindset was that they were better than blacks. It was a way of life for them in the south, and all of the blacks knew it. Even the police felt that way. I got a chance to find that out when I was about eight years old. This was before Mr. Green got Daddy out of prison, and we were living in Augusta, in a little house over by the city dump.

My mother was dating Arthur Jones, and he had been out on skid row and had gotten into a fight with some man that had cut him on the arm. He came home and my mother had bandaged him up to stop the bleeding. The next thing I knew, the police kicked the door down and hit Arthur upside the head with the butt of a pistol. They hit Arthur so hard until the pistol came out of the officer's hand and hit my mother on the chin. I remember my mother crying, as they handcuffed Arthur and took him off to jail. They didn't have a warrant, but like I said it was a way of life for them. They had a mindset that they were better than blacks. And believe it or not, as bad as that sounds, there was a time when it was even worse than that. Like the time when we first moved to Augusta and my mother moved out of my grandparents' house into an old house that used to be owned by a relative named Uncle Limb. So whenever that house was mentioned, it was always referred to as uncle Limb's house.

Mama had gotten on welfare, and one of the white women from social service came to the house one day. She wanted to inspect the house to see if Mama had a man living with her. So she was looking in the closet and under the beds to see if she could find a piece of man's clothing or a shoe or anything so they could cut her off welfare. They were not being realistic. They expected for a young woman in her twenties to not have a man in her life, no boyfriend or anything. They would cut you off before you could even try to explain that.

So intelligently you can see the circumstantial difference from back in that day until the time that we moved to the projects. Most importantly, I've noticed that when some black people think that just because they've achieved a little success that racism is almost or completely extinct. But to most of the blacks that are still living in poverty, racism is very much alive. Even to the point that it may seem it is never going to end. It's a feeling that I have had a many of times before.

The Way It Was

Finally, the day came that we were about to achieve the American dream, and owned our own home and move out of the projects. Daddy had applied for an FHA loan and was approved. We were building a three-bedroom brick house from the ground up. It was only going to be five houses down the street from my grandparents and only two houses down from the young man whom Cavan Smith had in that headlock. Remember when I said that everybody was kicking him so I kicked him too? Well as I looked back over my life, I realized that some of my best years were when we moved into that new brick house that we would come to know as home. We had come a long ways from living with one relative to the next, Little Dixie, Cotton Plant, and old houses that was hot in the summer and cold in the winter. We were in a new home, with all of the rooms having the same temperature. Not like many of the other old houses that we had lived in, most of which we had to heat with a woodstove if and when we had some wood. I can remember going out into the yard picking up the chips that was left over from when we had cut the logs down to size so that it would fit into the stove.

One day, Mama sent me outside to cut some firewood, and Warnell came out too. But I grabbed the axe first, and he wanted me to give him the axe, so in order for him to stop me from cutting the wood, he put his foot on the log. I kept telling him to move his foot and it was a double-bladed axe. I drew back and faked like I was going to come down with it. He would then snatch his foot back, I got tired of that. I

28

just wanted to cut the wood and go back in the house. He put his foot back on the log thinking that I was going to draw back and fake it again, but I didn't. This time, I came down with it and the axe landed right between his big toe and laid it wide open. Mama heard him when he screamed and looked out of the door, and when she saw all of the blood, she screamed. She didn't have time to whip me for rushing him to the doctor. This doctor's clinic was separated with blacks on one side and the whites on the other. On the blacks' side, there was no roof because they was still working on it, but even when it was finished, the black folks would be sweating and using whatever they had to fan with. And the water hydrant ran warm water. But on the white folks' side, they had air condition and cold water to drink. When Mama got back from the doctor's clinic, she was in no hurry to go anywhere else so she took her time and whipped me good, but I always felt that it was Warnell's fault.

Moving into the brick house meant that we had definitely come a long ways. The new house came with a lot of land. We had a big yard so my uncle Alvin put up a basketball hoop. If we were not in the house watching some kind of professional game like a Muhammad Ali fight, the World Series, NBA playoffs, or the Super Bowl, we would be outside playing basketball pretending to be pros. We built the house on the south end of town. This allowed for the boys on the north side to walk down to the south end just to play against us; it was the south side against the north. There were so many teams that you could not afford to lose because by the time you would be able to play again, you would have to wait until all of the other teams played before you would get another chance to play. Some of those games were so close they would go into triple overtime. People in Augusta are still talking about those games these days.

People used to come from all over just to watch us play. The young man that had become my best friend whose name was Willie Frank could not play ball all that good at first so nobody wanted to pick him on their team. But by he and I being best friends, of course, he always wanted me to pick him on my team, and that meant that I would have to work extra hard in order for us to win, and remember there were so many teams waiting for ups so we could not afford to lose. But Willie didn't give up, he kept trying and as you would know, he got to be pretty good; not as good as me of course, but at least the other teams would pick him from time to time. The Franks family was a lot like mine. They too had moved from Gregory to Augusta, and like us, they had bought a new house. It was a big family of them just like us. His family members were churchgoers, not like mine who only went to church sometimes, that nearly stayed in church. So, by he and I being best friends, I started to go all of the time too. I used to pass by that church and the grass would be all tall, there was a big padlock on the front door that could be seen from the street, and that was if the sunflowers that were about as tall as a building itself didn't block your view.

Willie introduced me to the pastor whose name was Jahir Dixon (Elder Dixon). He was a school teacher, a young man that didn't have a wife at that time, but was inviting people to church and telling them that the Lord had sent him to Augusta. Shortly after he moved to Augusta, some race-haters burned a cross in his yard. I can only guess that they thought that it would make him leave, but it didn't work. Now, next door to the right of us was a white family but we had no dealing with them as long as Daddy was home. But after living in the home for about eight years, one day Daddy just got up and left. He left my mom, he left us; and with him having the only income in the house, we were lost. It was like a nightmare, it just couldn't be happening. We were living better than we had ever lived. We were used to coming home and finding new clothes on our bed from time to time with all of the bills paid on time. But now it was very plain to see that we were in for some very difficult days ahead.

Mama had to swallow her pride by enlisting to welfare assistance. With almost the whole town talking "That's the lady whose husband left her." The white case worker acted like if the welfare would give you anything, it would come out of their pocket. And Mama was the type of person that would speak her mind to the white folks which was something that most blacks wouldn't do. So they looked up to Mama for that. After Daddy had been gone for about two years, Mama got involved with a man from the town of Newport, Arkansas, whose name was Eddie Giddy. Now Eddie was not as smart as Daddy was; as a matter of the fact, Eddie could not read or write. But he was willing to work. He would do little odds and ends jobs to help Mama pay the bills. Eddie had gotten in good with my uncles, plus they were kind of glad to see my mother with someone in her life since Daddy left. I can remember a few weekends where Eddie, my uncles, and my older brothers would be in a car setting out in the driveway late nights drinking, talking, and laughing out loud about a game or whatever they could make a conversation out of. Now, the white family that lived next door really didn't like blacks, especially the white lady. Her husband was not so bad, but he wouldn't socialize with us; however, occasionally he would give Eddie a cigarette just to get rid of him. Eddie was relentless with his knocking. The man had a habit of saying, "I'll give you one today, but I will not give you one tomorrow." They had a son who's going to move back home with them from Chicago, and his name was Mason Carter who had a drinking problem. He had a lot of money when he first came down to Augusta, but as time went by, he ended up broke. Although he was white and in the south, he was not prejudice because of the time he spent in Chicago living around blacks. So he became a good friend of the family, yet and still, the whites around there was not ready for blacks and whites to be equal.

One evening, just about dusk, I was at home cleaning up when there came a knock at the front door. It was Mason, who we had nicknamed Red. He had a lot of money, and it was the first time in a long time that he had a lot of money. He wanted a ride to the liquor store, so I stop what I was doing and gave him a ride to the liquor store. I borrowed Mama's old station wagon to take him. When we got to the liquor store, I stayed in the car because I was not old enough to buy. I was only sixteen years old, and you needed to be twenty-one to buy liquor in Arkansas, so knowing that I was not old enough, I just stayed in the car while Mason went inside. And on the way back home, we got pulled over by the police. My driver's license had expired, and I didn't have the money to renew them, and Red had loaded the back of the station wagon down with liquors and cases of beer. As bad as it may sound, we were so poor in those days until you could try to piece up enough money to get a drink from seven people and still fall short. So for Red to have bought

31

enough liquors and beers to last for two or three days, I couldn't wait to get back home and start drinking. Unfortunately, my luck ran out when the police pulled us over. I didn't have a valid driver's license, and I was underage with a car full of liquors and beers. Two policemen pulled us over, it was evident that they were playing good cop/bad cop, one of them was known among blacks to be a *redneck*.

Captain Linden Dirk was known as the redneck and Chief Grant Coldwater was known to show blacks some kindness from time to time. So the chief was telling me that he was going to just give me a ticket and let me take the car home but don't let him catch me driving again until I get my license renewed. Captain Linden Dirk said no. Red is going to jail for buying liquor for a minor, and I was going to jail for being a minor with liquor in the car while driving without a license. So Red and I went to jail, didn't even get to taste the liquor. The police took it all and kept it. There, we were in jail, Red got sick and started to shake real bad. Then the chief brought him a cup of liquor and passed it to Red through the jail bars. It was the first and only time that I had ever seen a policeman gave a man in jail a drink.

After about two days, I got out of jail. That was like the second time that I had been up to the Woodruff County Jail, the last time was about four months earlier when I was only sixteen and had just took my driver's test and passed it. I was just learning how to drive when I asked Willie's brother-in-law to let me drive his car to the store. He gave me the keys, and I left on my way to the biggest store in Augusta; the farther it was, the better because I wanted to drive. I got to the store, went in, and brought me something, feeling like a real man. I had finally got my driver's license. I drove myself to the store, and I was hoping that some of my classmates would see me and notice that I drove myself to the store.

I got out of the store and got in the car. I was looking to see who was noticing me as I went in reverse. Then there's a sudden boom as I backed up. It was the first day that I got my license, and the car I was driving wasn't even mine, it was Willie's brother-in-law. I had gotten into an accident already. And to make things worse, the car that I hit was the owner's of the store. The police came, took my driver's license, and gave me a ticket and a court date. I was only sixteen and I was terrified of going before a judge. My daddy was gone, and I didn't know what to do. I only had my license for one day and I had messed up. I didn't want to face that judge alone. I told my pastor Elder Dixon about what had happened and that I had a court date. Then he said to me, "Just let me know when your court date and I will go to court with you." When that day came, we went and the judge set up a payment plan. He wanted me to pay fifty dollars toward it that day. I didn't have any money so Elder Dixon paid it for me. I will be forever grateful for Elder Dixon. He was like a father to me.

Willie would come over to my house during the day, but I would hang out over to his house at night. Plus, I had a crush on his sister, Jazmin, and if I was lucky, I would get a glimpse of her every now and then before she and her sisters would go to bed.

Willie and I would stay up late especially on the weekends. We would be cooking popcorn, and sometimes we would be making biscuits. And when we didn't have any syrup then we would just make some homemade syrup out of sugar and water. And when we would be making a little bit too much noise, his mom or dad would yell from their bedroom, "It's time for y'all to go to bed." I knew just what that meant, it was time for me to go home.

And that was all right by Willie and me because we knew that I would be back tomorrow night. Occasionally, Willie would ease his parent's bedroom door close so that we didn't disturb them and that way I could stay over a little while. It was not much to do in Augusta other than to go to church, so sometimes we would just walk up and down the street in the front of our houses fantasizing about what we were going to have when we grow up. And because we went to church together, we were best friends and we could tell each other anything. He could tell me about things going on in his family that only family members knew. And I would do the same with him, and sometimes different family members would get jealous over our friendship, but we didn't care—we were friends. A part of our fantasy was that Willie and I were going to marry two sisters and my cousin Boomer was going to marry one of our wives' niece. I was going to live in New York, and we were going to be rich.

One night while Willie and I were walking someone called both of our names at the same time. We, of course, believed that it was the Lord. It was then that we realized that no man is able to call two different names at the same time. We were drum players for the church, and because there was nothing to do, most of the time we would hang out at the church playing drums. It only made sense for us to be good because we played all the time. Some of the girls from our class would come from the north end just to hear us play. And some of the boys that played in the school band would come and try to challenge us, but they were used to playing one drum and we were used to playing a whole set. We looked forward to going to the state convocation. The church had raised enough money to buy an old bus. And we could hardly wait to get on it and go to Little Rock. It was a big city and there was going to be lots of people there, especially girls.

Little Rock was a very big city compared to Augusta, and it would seem like a long trip there and back. It was one that we really enjoyed. After all, we only made that trip once a year. But that would soon change for me because I was about to leave my best friend and move to Little Rock to live with my real father. I was only five years old when I last saw him. I used to wonder about him; you know like what did he look like, was he rich, did he love me, did he care, or did he even miss me at all? After all, I was sixteen years old, and I didn't know much about him so I had to learn him and his ways. So there was a lot of catching up to do, as I had not seen him in all of those years. As soon as I walked up to him, he knew me right off the bat. He seemed to be just as glad to see me as I was to see him. And although I had a good stepfather, there is nothing like your own. And for the first time in a long time, I was not a stepchild, there were times when I heard my mom and my stepfather argue and in the heat of the argument Daddy would say to my mom, "You know that Kent ain't none of mine anyway." And as a child, I didn't understand that. I knew that he loved me but every time that they would get into it, he would throw me under the bus so to speak. It wasn't until I became a man when I realized that daddy was just trying to win the argument.

My real father had begun to teach me the things that he felt was very important for me to know. First, he wanted me to know my family history and how we got our last name. He said that my great great-grandfather was a slave on a plantation that was owned by the Murrays, and that my great great-grandfather was responsible for the supplies for the slaves. And he was good with fixing things so all of the slaves called him the handyman. So when slavery ended, most of the slaves signed out in the name of the plantation owner last name, but not my great great- grandfather, he signed out of slavery with his first and last name Handy Handy.

I learned that T. C. Cooper was a part of my family, and this gave me a sense of pride. T. C. Cooper was known as the father of the blues. I learned that my grandmother was a Choctaw native off the reservation in the state of Oklahoma. The land which the Little Rock International Airport was built on was once owned and farmed by my family, which was given to her by the government for Indian rights.

My father told me that he used to farm that land that is until he got bit by a cottonmouth moccasin and almost died. And would you believe that my grandmother healed him with an old Indian method, she gave him whiskey to drink and wrapped him up in blankets and made him sweat out the poison. My father got well and then left Little Rock by joining the United States Army; he fought in World War II. My grandmother had five sons and somehow they ended up in war at the same time, They all went overseas. As a matter of the fact, my dad said that he and his brother Uncle Major passed each other on deck of two passing warships in France. When my dad and uncles—Paul, Jacob, and Harry—got together and started talking about the war, they would tell the stories so real that if you close your eyes and use your imagination, you felt like you were there with them. My father served eight years in the United States Army, but my uncle Paul served twenty-two years. He fought in World War II and in the Korean conflict, and he would sometimes cry as he would tell the story. My father had been all around the world, and had met people from all walks of life. He had a broad outlook on life.

My mother had done a good job raising me, but there are just some things that a boy needs to get from his father. I asked my father once what happened to him and my mother, and he said that it was just that my mother wanted to move back to that small town. He just couldn't live in a small town where everybody knows everybody's business, and a place where blacks still had to go into white-owned businesses through the backdoor.

Like I had said earlier, there was a lot of catching up to do. Daddy had told me that he also had six other kids that lived in Kansas City, Kansas. And that he wanted me to get to know them, so he arranged for me to go to Kansas City to meet them.

They were two brothers and four sisters whom I never even knew that I had. So I stayed in Kansas City for a while, and we got to know each other and form a close bond. Their mother became my mother, and then I moved back to Little Rock with my dad and the following summer with my brother William Jr., who also came from Kansas City and lived with our dad.

We attended school at Hall High School, which was an open-campus school. It was like going to college, you could leave school after class, and you didn't have to be back until your next class. I pretty much didn't know how to act in a school like that. I surely couldn't do that in Augusta, but William Jr. and I would go to Augusta on some weekends. By then, I had introduced him to my mother's side of the family, and I would be telling my brothers on my mother's side about just how different school was in Little Rock from the schools in Augusta. So they started coming to Little Rock to hang out with William Jr. and I. They would visit my school, but they never attended it. My uncle Johnny's oldest son Leon, who we had nicknamed Boomer, and my aunt Nellie's only son Otis would also come to what was at that time a big city to hang out with us. Especially considering coming from a small town like Augusta, and although Boomer and Otis were my first cousins, they really were more like brothers to me because we were so close. And if we were not touring the city, we would be up late nights listen to Daddy telling us about the war and sometimes he would be telling us about things that he had experience while he was in different parts of the world. I might add that he had jokes for days. After that, I had graduated from Hall High School, and I started dating a young lady that was living in Augusta, she moved there from Saint Louis.

Keep on Swimming

I moved back home with my mother, but I would still go to Little Rock from time to time to check on my dad. But now that I had finished school, it was time to reunite with my best friend Willie Frank and my other cousins, the bebe kids, in order to get back into the swing of things. Things hadn't changed much since I had left and came back, the blacks still had to go to the White River to swim, and with a name like the White River, I am surprise that they allowed us to do that.

On one hot summer day, we did just that. I owned a car, so I had taken two carloads of people down the river to swim. First, I had taken the adults and then the young people, now sometimes in order for the boats and grain barges to get through they would have to dig the bottom of the river out. They would take the sand that they would dig out from the bottom of the river and put it on the banks making it like a beach. And since we didn't have anywhere else to go to swim, we would take advantage of that. So we swim and swim that day and because they had not yet finished digging, we noticed in a distance some white guys in the middle of the river on a boat who were stuck on a sand bed, but they were walking around in water that was about waist-deep. They were drinking, cussing, and talking aloud, and those white guys were known to hate blacks. It was getting dark and time to pack up and go. We definitely didn't want to be down there at nightfall, and because I had two carloads of people down there, I knew I was going to have to make two trips taking everybody back. So I started with the adults first and then one of my cousins from the bebe tribes, who we had nicknamed

Fox, went with me to drop off the adults. Then we headed back to get the rest of the young people, but when we got back there, everyone was gone except for those white guys out in the middle of the river.

Fox said to me, "Do you want to hit it again real quick before we leave?"

I responded, "I don't care."

We dived in and in just a few minutes in the water, I felt something brush up against my leg so I told Fox that I was getting out. So we swam to the bank and got out and went home. But what we didn't know, but found out about the next day, when I went down to my grandparents, my grandmother asked me did they ever find Ms. Lena's son? I didn't know what she was talking about. I hadn't heard that he was even missing. Then she said that they think that he is in that river, and then Warnell began to say, "Yesterday, while yawl was gone to take people home, somebody came down to the river in a truck and gave us a ride home, but on our way back, we saw Agustin. We told him that there weren't anybody else down there but them white boys, and he waved at us, smiled, turned around, and went down there."

Later on that same day, they found Agustin's body in the White River with his fist balled up and a knot on his forehead.

Everybody knew that the white guys had did it. Agustin couldn't and didn't swim for years. We had tried to get Agustin to get in the water or to let us teach him how to swim, and he wouldn't. They found Agustin's body right where Fox and I were swimming at. As a matter of fact, I believe that was Agustin's body that brushed up against my leg. Nothing ever became of it. Nobody spent a single night in jail for it, it was just another day in Woodruff County. There was a lot of talk in the black community about Agustin being murdered, but that's all that it was, just blacks talking among themselves. No one would dare stand up to a white man and say anything to him that they were saying to one another.

Those of us who were used to swimming in the White River had heard the old story years ago. There was a sawmill on the banks of the White River, and how that a worker fell into the river one day and that the man didn't know how to swim. Some divers were called in from

Little Rock to find his body. Legend has it that instead of the divers finding his body, when they went down to the bottom of the river, they saw a catfish as big as a Volkswagen, but the man's body was never found. However that didn't stop us from swimming in it although we have had a couple of close calls ourselves. For instance, on one hot summer day, we were down there at the river swimming, and I had finally talked Oscar into letting me teach him how to swim. Oscar and I had become really good friends, so he trusted me; unlike Agustin who would never get in the water. I took Oscar into my arms, and started to walk backwards into the river. My intentions were to hold him up while he paddles until he got the hang of it and be able to stay afloat on his own. But instead while I was dragging him up in my arms, all of a sudden there was no more earth under my feet.

We went underwater without a chance to take a deep breath. Oscar panicked. It was like a bottomless drop off when we were going down. I was trying to push Oscar forward toward the bank so that all he would have to do was stand up and I could have swum back in. But I could not get his arm from around my neck. I was running out of air and had started to take in water. I was drowning, and there was nothing that I could do about it. There were so many of us in the water I wasn't sure if anybody had even noticed that we were under. Then just when I thought that it was over for me, I felt someone come up from behind me and give me a big push toward the bank. It was just enough for my toes to touch some ground. You're talking about a "toe holt," meaning barely touching the ground with your feet. Let me tell you, I mean that literally. And who was it that gave Oscar and I the push that saved our lives? It was none other than Cavan Smith the same boy that I told you had Willie in that headlock when I first went to school in Woodruff County. I'm forever grateful to Cavan for that. I made it to the bank and threw Oscar off my neck, and I never tried to teach him how to swim again. Like I said, we had some close calls before, and swimming in a river is just plain ole dangerous. Agustin's death was a horse of a different color; everyone knew that he would never get in the water. It wasn't until some years later when we would understand and realize that Agustin's death was just the first of many blacks that would be murdered in Woodruff County.

I had met and fell in love with the young girl that had moved to Augusta from Saint Louis, and she was living with her grandmother, who at first seemed to like me. But then for no apparent reason, she started to act like she hated me. She even went as far as to say that she was going to send my girlfriend to a foster home. I didn't want that to happen but I was told that the only way that I could stop it was to get married. The only problem with that was I was twenty-one and she was only sixteen. I went around her grandmother to her mother and asked for her hand in marriage, and her mother signed the papers giving me permission to marry her. On August 24, 1981, we got married. We were living at home with my mother, and a good job was hard to find, I mean I could find little odds and ends jobs. But now that I had a wife to support, I needed to have something steadier. So I went and join the Army National Guard, my oldest brother had just finish his six years and got out with an honorable discharge. When he found out that I had join, sworn in, and was waiting on my orders to report to active duty, he came and gave me a few pointers of what to and not to do. But sadly what I didn't know at the time that I joined was that you could be anything that you want to be in the army. I thought that everybody had to lie in the woods and fight in the mud and water; I didn't know that you could be a police, a cook, a doctor, or anything. Gladly I didn't join by myself, but also a young man that stayed a few houses down from my grandparents. He was a south ender also, and he used to play ball with us all the time. His name was Victor Lee Roberson, but we nicknamed him Ray Bo. Not only did he join with me, but we went in on what was called a buddy system. That meant that we would fly out on the same day, go the same places, be in the same company, and stay in the same barracks all the way through basic training. We got our orders in the mail to report to duty on October 18, 1982. I had never flown before, but Ray Bo had. The closest I had ever been to an airplane was when I had moved to Little Rock and would walk down to the end of my block to the landing strip of the Bill and Hillary Clinton National Airport and watch the planes land and take off. So quite naturally, Ray Bo was trying to comfort me about the flight, seeing that I had a lot of concerns about the flight. The flight attendant gave us the instruction that the plane hits the runway and lifts off the ground and it was not as bad as I thought that it would be.

We were on our way to Fort Jackson, South Carolina. One of the most impressive things about it was that it was night when we left the ground, but once we got about the clouds, it was still day. We were in Fort Jackson for three days for orientation. On the first night, we were being told where we would be sleeping. They were also telling us not to try to run away, because one boy had tried to do that, and he was found dead in the woods, which Fort Jackson just happens to be surrounded by them. The next night, I was awaken to some noise of lockers being slammed, and people were talking there were some new recruits; their flight had just landed so they were putting their things away in the lockers. I thought to myself now that I'm up I may as well use the bathroom, so I got up and went in. There they were, some new guys in there talking, but they were speaking Spanish. They were Puerto Ricans form New York City; it was definitely something that you don't see every day in Augusta.

We introduced ourselves, and I went back to bed. But as the days followed, we would meet up and talk. We spent a lot of time talking about how different New York City was from Arkansas, and I was amazed at what they were telling Ray Bo and me. I had already said that I wanted to live in New York way back when I was just a young boy walking the streets of Augusta fantasizing. And now hearing them talk about New York just made me want to live there even more. Again as faith would have it, we all left Fort Jackson after three days of orientation and went to Fort Benning, Georgia. We would all go to the same barracks and become the best of friends. We arrived at Fort Benning on October 22, 1982. I often refer to that day as "twenty-two, twenty-two" because it was on my twenty-second birthday. It was October 22, and I turned twenty-two years old that day, and what a birthday to remember. It took us about two weeks before we were able to write back home. It was about that long before you would even know your new address.

My wife had made a doctor's appointment before I left to see if she was pregnant. She was to go to the doctor on Monday, but my orders were to leave on Sunday. I left a day before her appointment, and it had been two weeks since we last talked. It was my twenty-second birthday, they bused us from the airport to the base, and as soon as the bus pulled up and came to a stop, the drill sergeants got on the bus and said to us, "You got three seconds to get off of this bus, and two of them are already gone." People were so scared, they were running over one another trying to get off of that bus, they were working us like we were prisoners of war. I finally got a chance to write home with my new address.

Although I had started basic training on my birthday, it all wasn't bad, because she wrote me back and said that she went to her appointment and that she was pregnant. So I started to tell all of the fellows the good news, then Victor Lee Robertson, who we had nickname Ray Bo, told me that he had been dating my sister Vanessa and that she was also pregnant with their first child. At that time, it was too early in my wife's pregnancy to know whether if she was having a boy or girl. Yes, the little boy that used to hang at the café had finally become a man. I was about to be a father. One day, we were outside polishing our boots when it came time for mail call, and they called my name because I got mail. It was a letter from my wife saying that we were having a boy. And since it was my first child, I named him after me, Kent Lemont Handy Jr. We were about halfway through basic training by December, so Ray Bo and I went home for Christmas. By then, my wife was well along in her pregnancy, and she was showing real good. So, in order to stay in shape, we had to run while we were on break to keep from gaining weight from all of the holiday cooking and eating. After the holidays, we left and went back to Fort Benning to finish AIT (Advanced Infantry Training). Ray Bo had started to get into trouble with fighting and all of that. One day, he was lying across his bed when the company commander came into the barracks, and everybody went to attention. Well, everybody but Ray Bo that is, he had on some headphones listening to his music, and he had his locker wide open with a *Playboy* magazine showing; we were not allowed to have such things. So the company commander simply just walked over to Ray Bo's radio and turned it up to what looked like as loud as it could get. Then Ray Bo immediate thought that one of the guys did it and jumped up ready to fight. That is until he realized that it was the company commander who did it, so Ray Bo got an Article 15 for that and instead of taking money or rank from him, he was made to pull extra duty on weekends. The drill sergeants would tell us during the week that they were going to give us an off-post weekend pass. But every time that it would get close to the weekend, they would find some kind of reason or make up some kind of excuses to say that we were not going to get a pass. But our platoon leader was a college student named Charlie; he was from Boston, Massachusetts, and he wrote a letter to the company commander telling him about us not getting any off-post pass. It didn't do any good because by the time that they responded to it, we were about ready to graduate. So, there we would clean our weapons while other soldiers from the other platoons passed by on their way with an off-post pass. Although, this happened the whole time that we were in training, we never got an off-post pass.

The most that we were able to do was to go the PX (a store on base). Ray Bo had to work on weekends. I would go and see him and sneak him a few beers. I used to smoke when I first got there, but they cut us down to just one a day. One day, after training, the drill sergeants left, and I decided to go out on the back porch and have me another cigarette. And as soon as I lit it up and took me a couple of puffs of it, the drill sergeant came from what looked like out of nowhere, and to me, "What do you think you're doing? Don't you know that somebody else done already tried to do this even before you even joined the army? Throw that cigarette away and get inside." I quit smoking altogether after that. One night, the drill sergeant, who was on duty told the soldier that was keeping guard duty to go and get me and tell me to come here. So he woke me up and said that the drill sergeant wanted to see me, and I can remember thinking what did I do wrong to make the drill sergeant wake me up out of my sleep this time of night? Whatever it is it's got to be bad. But when I got to the office, the drill sergeant said to me that he had been noticing me, and that he had also notice how the other guys look up to me. He wanted me to tell them to stop playing around so much and to get serious about what they were trying to teach us because it could make the difference between dying and staying alive in the event of a war. The drill sergeant went on to say that we had been in training long enough to march in time, but that we were still marching off beat, in other words we were not keeping step. After he finished talking to me, I went back to the barracks, and a lot of the guys wanted to know what that was all about. What had I done? What did the drill sergeant want with me that was so important that it could not wait until morning? I noticed that they looked up to me and since a lot of them were awake already, I had the talk with them right then and there. And just like he had said, they listened to me and in just a few days, we were marching in step.

My oldest brother Joe had already told me two rules to always remember: One of them was to never volunteer for anything in the army because it may not be what you think. He said that one time, the army asked them if there were any people to volunteer to drive trucks. He and some others said yes and then they gave them some wheelbarrows to push. The second rule was the less that the drill sergeant knows your name the better off you would be. And guess what, he was right, once that the drill sergeant learns your name, they would use you for an example. For instance, like they did the Benjamin brothers that were from Chicago. The drill sergeant were always on them about something; if it wasn't about one thing, it would be another. Those guys were from Chicago, and they used to talk back and make smart remarks to the drill sergeants. They were very negative and it was hard to motivate them, they gave the drill sergeants a hard time. But when it came time for us to go into the gas chamber, they had us to all line up along the wall and the drill sergeants blocked the exits then they told us to unmask and say our name rank and serial number, and then they would let us out. But when it came time for the brothers, they made them stay extra long. By the time that they let them out, they had a string of snot hanging from their chin down to their feet. With the exits blocked, they had to almost fight to get out to fresh air. I realized that I was doing good right before we went home for Christmas when Ray Bo and I went to the office to give the drill sergeant a gift. It was a wristwatch, and although he told us that the drill sergeants were not supposed to receive gifts for soldiers, he was touched. And then he asked us our names. That was the magic moment we had only a few weeks left, and he didn't even know our names. We did it. We did just what my oldest brother had told us to do. And that was to remember rule number two: Don't do anything that would make the drill sergeants remember your name. One of the guys that we had met at Fort Jackson and became good friends with was Noah. He was one of the guys that was telling us about New York City. We had become the best of friends we could tell each other anything, and boy did we have some fun; we would laugh some time until we cry. One night we had a night exercise, and we were supposed to stop a team from overrunning us in an ambush, but Noah, Ray Bo, and I dug us a three-man foxhole and padded it with some of those Georgia pines that fell from the trees. We then put our sleeping bags down in the foxhole, got in them, zipped them up, and went to sleep. While everybody else was running around shooting and throwing bombs, man we laughed about that the next day for a long time. It is something about going through hard times with someone. You bond with them and it makes you special to each other. Finally, after a five-mile run, a fifteen-mile road march, and all of the other requirements that the United States Army had, we graduated. And when we had got to the airport, we had a toast to the good times and to each other for graduating because everybody who started out with us didn't make it through. We all then hugged, said our good-byes, and went our separate ways. So Ray Bo and I were on our way back to Augusta, but some of our friends were going to Fort Bragg for jump school.

We returned from training on January 10, 1983, but by then I was so hyped up until I tried to go full-time army. I wanted to get out of the guard and serve full-time army, but they would not allow me; they said that it was because they were understaffed and needed every man. But if I could wait for one year then I could go full-time army, I had gotten used to being a soldier every day, not just one weekend a month. You talking about killing your morale waiting all month to be a soldier was definitely a drag. Plus, I had gotten used to a nice paycheck. Since being back home and in the guard, my pay dropped from eleven hundred to only eighty- eight dollars a month. We were living with my mom and out of my eighty-eight dollars, I tried to give my mom something even if it was no more than twenty dollars. With a wife and baby to support, my finances became really restricted.

If that wasn't bad enough, my mother was losing her home to foreclosure, and she showed me a letter that said that she had to be out of the house by January 17. That meant that we only had seven days to find somewhere else to move. I could hardly believe it, I am just getting home from all of that hard training, and we are losing our home that we had built from the ground up. And we only got a week to find somewhere to move before the sheriff would be coming by to put us out and sit our things on the side of the road. As far back as I can remember, I have never known the sheriff to sit anybody in Augusta out on the street. I definitely didn't want our family to be the first so I told my mother to just let them have that house because if we got put out by the sheriff, it would be an embarrassment to the town. We had been a family that was well respected in that town, but now we were racing against time to beat the embarrassment. Although we beat the deadline on getting out of the house, we still had a certain level of embarrassment. Because with only a week to find somewhere else to go and with just a few dollars saved, we had to get what we could find just to keep from being homeless. So we found a house at 505 Fifth Street. It was an old house that needed a whole lot of work. No one had lived there for a long time, it used to belong to an old relative, but when he died, the family lost it due to taxes. So it was now owned by one of the white lawyers in town.

My mother went and talked to him, and he rented it to her. The house was condemned and Mom didn't have but a few dollars, and I only had a few dollars too. We were not able to afford to hire someone to fix it like it needed to be fixed. But we were blessed because my uncles were carpenters, so we got the materials and they did the work. This house was in such bad shape they even had to put in new floors. It even had holes in the ceiling; one of which I patched with a cardboard box. Like I said, although we beat the deadline to keep the sheriff from sitting us and our things out, we were still embarrassed because of what we had to move to. We had gone form a new brick home that we had built from the ground to an old condemned house that needed lots of work. Although it was a setback, we had been there many times before, and that is one of the reasons I believe that it is very important that you don't forget where you came from.

Relentless Struggle

My best friend Willie and his family still had their house, but word got around that Daddy had quit his job and left my mom and us. And because Daddy had built the house in his name, only when Mama went to apply for welfare, the FHA found out about it, and foreclosed on the house. We had lived in that brick house for ten years and some of the kids had never lived in that old house before. Everybody that was ten and under had never lived in an old house. As a matter of fact, we could go back as far as thirteen years considering the projects, which also was a new brick house. So to move into an old house with some of the rooms being warm and others being cold made it really hard for them to get used to. Although they had experienced some difficult times before; for instance, while we were yet in the brick house, Mama was getting some high utility bills. She had the light company to come to the house to find out why, and they came to the conclusion that it was because of the water heater. Mama had them disconnect it so the kids had to wash up in cold water before attending school.

Although Mama had them disconnect the water heater, the bills still kept coming high, and at the time that they had the brick house built, they had it to be built an all-electric house because the contractor told them that it was going to be the wave of the future and it was going to be cheaper than gas. But still the bills kept coming high, so again Mama asked the utility company to come and find the cause, and this time, they said that it was because of the air conditioner that was in the window. With the bills still coming high, Mama thought that perhaps it was time for her to go down to the utility company and have a little talk with them. The secretary was telling Mama that her bills were high because of that water heater and air conditioner. The utility bills at the brick house were in Daddy's middle name, they didn't even know that we had moved.

When Mama informed her that we no longer lived in the brick house, the bills began to drop. However, the problem was that Mama was only getting $202 a month from welfare. Unfortunately, each month she was still in a struggle. She had to buy things for the house, her personals, and pay whatever bills that she could with limited financial resources. It was not hard to see that everything was getting out of control. She just didn't have enough money to pay all of the bills. It was like a cycle, each month she would only pay a portion of her utility bill. She didn't have enough money to pay the whole bill in full, so the balance of each bill would go over to the next month. Until eventually she was not able to pay the utility bill at all. Then the light was cut off, and since the Augusta light company was privately owned, they could pretty much do whatever they wanted to. Meaning that they could take a parcel payment if they liked you, or they could demand payment in full also when your lights got cut off; that meant that your gas and water would be cut off as well. So can you imagine what it must have been like to have gone from a brick house to an old condemned house that needed a lot of work, and on top of all of that, we were in the dark without drinking water or heat.

To escape the misery, we would separate and go and stay with our kinfolks; some of us would stay with our grandparents. Mostly the younger kids but us older kids would stay with our aunt Charlotte and her kids, you know the bay bays, until Mama could get the money up by borrowing it from some of her family members. They would lend her just enough money to get the lights back on, and after about two or three months, depending on how much the utility bills would be, the lights would be off again. And this happened from January 1983 to February 1984. The light company would give you until the fifteenth of each month to pay your bill. Mama already knew by the first of February that she was not going to be able to pay her light bill by the fifteenth so we were already bracing ourselves to be in the dark again. But on the morning of February 16, we heard that it was a program in Cotton Plant that was helping people with their utility bills. And we knew that the lights were going to get cut off sometime today because Mama didn't pay by the fifteenth. So Mama and I went down to Cotton Plant early that morning on February 16, 1984, and because of the crowd, we had to wait in line all day. Finally, it was our time and Mama was telling them about our situation. I would only say something when and if I thought that it was important for them to know. After a long day waiting, the lady said that based on Mama's income, she was eligible for the help. So immediately we thought finally bits of good news. We won't have to be in the dark after all. The lady from the program called Augusta light company to ask them not to turn off Mrs. Armstrong utilities because she was qualified for the help and that a check would be put in the mail that day. However, the secretary reported that if the check wasn't on her desk by the end of the day then Mama's lights would be turned off.

We had been down there all day, it was now after three o'clock. The Augusta light company closed at five o'clock. We realized at that time that in spite of our best efforts we were still going to be in the dark. Now Mama and I had already stopped by the light company early that morning before we left for Cotton Plant to make a plea for them to not turn off our lights. But the secretary said to my mom, "We're going to teach you a lesson." Not really knowing just what she meant by that, we went on to Cotton Plant. Although it was only thirty some miles from Cotton Plant to Augusta, it seem like a long, deserted, emotional drain ride back to Augusta. Back to an old house that in just a matter of minutes was going to be dark and cold. After all, it was February 16. Shortly after we arrived back at the house, sure enough they came and turned off the utilities again. We were tired, tired of having to go and stay with kinfolks, tired of borrowing money just to end up in the same old situation, tired of being embarrassed and to fall from a respected family in town to having to gather up all of the pots and milk jugs that you could find and go and knock on our neighbor's door and ask if you could have some water. And to keep from warning out our welcome, we would go to different houses in the neighborhood to ask if we could have some water.

This went on from February 16 until March 1, and unlike other times, we had made up our minds that we were not going to stay with kinfolks, but stay in that cold dark house that we had come to know as home. The kids were scared and afraid to sleep in any of the bedrooms in the back of the house as long as the utilities were off so they would sleep in Mama's room whose bedroom was in the front of the house. Come to think about it, nobody slept in any of the back bedrooms of the house as long as the lights were off. We, the older kids, stayed up all night in the living room telling jokes and laughing until daybreak then we would go to bed and sleep during the day while we had daylight, this went on for those sixteen days. Our friends used to come home with us after the club because they knew we would still be up cooking and telling jokes. So just because the lights were off didn't stop anything; it was common to pass by our house at three or four o'clock in the morning and hear someone laughing out loud even though we would try hard not to get too loud because we knew that the kids still had to go to school.

If we still had some of the cold water left over that we asked then that's what they would wash up in for school; and without any gas, they couldn't as much as cook an egg for breakfast. On February 28, 1984, Eddie Giddy, who was my mother's boyfriend at the time, decided to go and work with a man named Whisper Dooley. Eddie had the truck and Whisper had the chain saws. Their plan was to go to the woods, cut down some trees, cut them up into firewood, and sell it to make money, and since Augusta was the kind of town that a lot of people used woodstoves, it wasn't a bad idea. There was just one small problem—Whisper Dooley was a known Ku Klux Klan member. My mother had told Eddie to be very careful dealing with Whisper. Because she remembers when she was just a young girl living in Gregory seeing Whisper dressed out in his Klan outfit. So even though we needed some money real bad, working with Whisper was not something that Mama was willing to do. Mama has always been the kind of person who would help anybody as much as she could, which was the reason why she allowed a young man that we had nicknamed Choppy to live with us. Both of his parents were dead, so Mama took him in, and since she was doing that entirely, she knew how to do to get the lights back on. She thought that maybe if she would send Choppy up to the light company with a partial payment that they might take it especially since his last name was different from ours. When

Choppy came back, and he that it was rejected, and they were not going to take a partial payment for that address.

Minutes later, a light company truck pulled up in front of the house and an obese white guy got out of the truck and went to the side of the house. Mama and I were standing in the front door with the door wide open, waiting to see why he was there. And then he came back to the truck with the whole gas meter in his hand, and he put it in the back of the truck and left. It was as if they were mad at Mama for sending Choppy up there. I recognize the obese white guy. It was Jeff Row Cox, a classmate of mine and a racist. I had already hit him upside his head once in the eighth grade for calling me the "n" word. But I didn't know that he had gotten a job with the city light company. Ironically, I later found out that the secretary of the light company, who my mother had been having words with, was his mother. I think that it would be safe to say that his mother had something to do with him getting that job with the city light company. Have you ever had a strange feeling, but you just didn't know what it was? You know, the kind of feeling when you know that something isn't right but you just can't put your finger on it.

My uncle Thomas and his wife both worked and needed someone to babysit, so they asked my wife if she would do it. She said yes but it was still cold outside, and with her having to get up early and take our baby out in the cold every morning wasn't good. So they told us, "Why doesn't yawl just stay over our house, and that way you'll already be here in the morning." It sounded good to me. At least they had lights so we did. My cousin Fox, who was one of the bebe kids, stayed right across the street from my uncle, and he asked me if I wanted to do some work with him in the morning. On the morning of March 1, I got up and went to work for a guy cutting up chicken wire. I tore my newest pair of pants my wife had gotten me for an anniversary gift. When we finished, the man only paid us about fifteen dollars, which wasn't even enough to pay for the pants that I had torn up. I was very disappointed. I went by Mama's to get a change of clothes. When I got there, only Mama, Kizzie, who was her baby, and Otis, who was my first cousin who was more like a brother to me and my aunt Nellie's only son, were there. I asked where the other kids were, and Mama said that they gone up to my wife's aunt's house to see my son. They loved him and always wanted to hold and kiss on him, they would be saying, "It's my turn to hold him." Kent Jr. was only a year and a few months old at the time. Otis was sitting in a chair in Mama's room, but he had a real sad look on his face, which was so not him, because he was the type of guy that always had a smile. So I started to tease him about some money, after all, it was March 1, and Otis's mother was getting a check for him too. I thought that he would have some money like he normally would on the first, but he just looked at me with that sad face and said that "me check didn't come today." So I stopped teasing him seeing that he was not in the mood.

Mama started to tell me about Whisper Dooley and how that he had come by the house last night with a pistol in one hand and a flashlight in the other, looking for Eddie and saying that he came to kill him. I asked what for, and she said that she was not sure but he said something about a maul. I then asked her if she called the police, and she said no. She was lying across her bed as she was telling me about Whisper and the reason why she didn't want Eddie to work with Whisper Dooley in the first place. Mama said that she had been to the doctor because she was not feeling good and that the doctor had told her that she had too much stress on her and that whatever she was worrying about she needed to just let it go, because it was about to give her a stroke or a heart attack. She went on to say that she was not going to worry anymore about paying any bills, but that she had already told the kids that she was going to move out of Augusta. And move to Newport where Eddie's parents lived. She said that the kids were very happy, had started to pack up their things, and had made plans about going to the park there because Newport had a park and Augusta didn't. I agreed with Mama that she had to stop worrying about any bills and that leaving Augusta was a good idea and that she could get a fresh start. I also told her that we had lost everything else and that all we had left was each other. I started to walk out of Mama's room to go into my bedroom to get a change of clothes. In between the two rooms was a hallway, and I noticed that in the ceiling of the hallway was a big hole. I knew that it was there. Like I had said before, the old house needed a lot of work, but this was the hole that I had already put a piece of cardboard over for a temporary fix.

But now it was wide open, so I yelled, "Who done tore down the cardboard from this hole here in the hallway?"

Mama yelled back to me and said that Gina did it. She had told Ryan to look up into the hole. It was nothing more than an attic, but Gina wanted Ryan to see what was up there. She told Ryan that because this house was so old that maybe someone had hid a trunk full of money up there. Then Mama said to me, "I wish you would've been here when Ryan looked up there. He came down trembling, and I asked him what was wrong, and he said that he saw four caskets stacked on top of each other." Then Mama said that Gina told Ryan to look again because it could have been a trunk, and so he did, but this time when he came down, he said that he saw a white doll with a rope around its neck and that the doll looked at him and just hung its head. Mama said that Ryan started to beg Gina to please don't make him look up there anymore. So I made Gina leave him alone said Mama, and I made the reply that Gina was crazy and went on into my room. Then that feeling came again. You know, the one when you know that something was wrong but you just can't put your finger on it. I looked around in my room as if it was going to be the last time I was going to ever see it. Immediately, I started grabbing up all of my best clothes then I caught myself, and I put them all back down except for a shirt and a pair of pants.

I was going to go back over to my uncle's house to take a bath and change my clothes. I stopped and stood at the door to Mama's room.

I asked Otis was he going out tonight and he said, "No, I don't have any money." But then he said to me, "If this house would ever catch fire, I know where I would get out at."

I asked, "Where?"

He said, "Right there," as he was pointing at a crack in the wall over by Mama's closet.

I just smiled and left. My mother later told me that while Otis was yet sitting in her room, he said to her, "Aunt Paul, something strange is going to happen and it's going to shock the whole world, and you going to get a trunkful of money behind it."

The Incident

I had finished my bath and got dressed. I went out to Jerry's café, where my brother Dwayne was the DJ and a guy by the name of Logan Jack Brown. Everybody call him Logan Jack; he was a friend of the family, because my oldest brother Joe married Logan's oldest sister. But this was a Thursday night known as lady's night. It was the 1st of March 1984, and Logan Jack Brown had a little too much to drink that he broke the glass on the jukebox. So the owner put him out. On his way home, he decided to stop by our house. My mother and Eddie were gone to an auction alone with my aunt Charlotte, who was the mother of the bebes, and my sisters Vanessa and Shelia, who had borrowed Otis's new Colt. Gina had said that she was not going anywhere, so Mama left her to watch the kids but, after Mama had left, Gina changed her mind because one of her girlfriends came by and ask her to go out with her so Gina decided to go out. And with the kids been left alone in that cold, dark house, one can only imagine how scared they were, and one can only imagine how glad they must have been to see Logan Jack.

Ryan asked Logan Jack to stay there with them until Mama got back from the auction. He also told Logan Jack Brown that he had seen three white men in Mama's backyard, so Logan Jack looked out of the window and saw them, but he could not make out who they were. Logan Jack Brown said that he got up and went outside and around the back of the house but that he didn't see anybody. But according to Richard, James Logan Jack did see them and talked to them too; they supposedly asked him if Eddie was home, and Logan Jack either said yes, he was not sure, or maybe he said that he just didn't know.

There was a shed that sit between our house and the house next door. When Logan Jack got up to go outside, the kids were terrified and was begging him not to leave them. I believed that his intentions were to check it out and come back in the house, but I believed that when those white guys asked him if Eddie was home regardless of what his answer was, they told him to leave. And he did just what they said. He didn't know them, but he did know that they were policemen, and like most people, he did what the police told him to do. He left the kids there terrified all alone, and the reason that he didn't recognized those policemen were because they were not from Augusta but were from Patterson— they were Patterson police. After they had gotten to Augusta, they parked their police cars at the Augusta Fire Department, and these are the facts. There was no legal reason for them to even be in Augusta especially at that time of night.

Meanwhile those three had made their way down to my mother's house, and had been there long enough to make Logan Jack leave. And as the Augusta policeman was making his rounds, he realized that the Patterson police cars are at the Augusta Fire Department, but no one is inside, so he called a dispatcher to report it, and this was at 12:01 a.m. And these are facts. I believe that the rest took place like this, the three white Patterson policemen decided to go in the house. After that, they told Logan Jack to leave, it would have been easy to get in through the front door. After all, they were the police. There was a knock at the front door. The kids thought that it's Logan Jack coming back in so they simply yell, "Come in the door open," but it's not Logan Jack, so fear fell upon them. It was some white faces they had never seen before, and they happen to be the police. They are scared because they are policemen but they are terrified because they are white, they don't recognize any of them, and they are in the only place in the world that they got to call home. They were asking where Eddie Giddy was and were making jokes about living in a house without lights or gas, while the others are searching the rest of the house looking for Eddie. They realized that the kids are alone. After that, those who were searching came back and said,

"There's no one else in the house." They got mad because they missed Eddie. And Tracy has just responded to their jokes and told them to get out of her mother's house.

It dawned on them there are no lights, and no one even knew that we were here, and there was no one else here with us. "We could kill these "n" word and get away with it." Tracy was thirteen, so one of the officers grabbed her to tear off her clothes to expose her breast and to rape her. She started screaming, and he started choking her to keep her quiet, but she is screaming in agonizing fear. The policeman thought to himself this is an assault, and she has seen my face, so he takes out a pocketknife and stabbed her. All the rest of the kids saw it, and they started running and hollering for help to the top of their little lungs, because they know that this is real, and I don't want to die. I want to see my mother again. It's a matter of life and death, but by yelling, they realized that they were giving away their positions where they were hiding, so they kept quiet, but the policemen knew that they have gone too far to stop now. The other policemen locked the doors. Tracy was dying and the other kids knew that they also knew that they couldn't get out, and that if those policemen find them that they were going to kill them too. They were hiding in the other rooms. The same rooms that they were afraid to sleep in while the lights were off, which was the main reason that they would sleep in Mama's room in the first place. It was a ten-room house. With no lights, the policemen knew they needed to do something because there was a good chance that someone else heard all of that screaming, running, things being knocked over, and yelling.

The secretary of the fire department was their connection. It was him that told them that when they got to Augusta they could park and leave their police cars at the fire station. Feeling that someone may have heard something, they knew that they could not use their flashlights to look for the hiding kids. So one of the officers called down to the store where the secretary worked at to tell him that they were going to need some gas to finish the job. He already knew what was happening from the meeting that they had at the whites-only club. But while he was on the phone with them telling him that they needed some gas, my mother walked in. They were back from the auction. She needed some batteries for a battery-operated light that she had brought at the auction that she was so sure that the kids would be glad to have and use. She noticed him on the phone, and him looking at her like he has just seen a ghost. Mama noticed the way he looked at her and his strange behavior. Then he turned his back to her to finish the conversation. Meanwhile, Otis changed his mind about going out and asked my uncle to give him a ride up to Mama's house to see if Shelia was back with his new Colt. So my uncle said that he was getting ready to go to the store anyways, so he would just drop him off about a block away from the house. And so he did, and Otis walked on to the house and knocked on the door. To his surprise, no one answered, so he just turned the knob, and went inside like he had so many times before. But he didn't know that the policemen were inside the house hiding ever since he first knocked on the door.

When he gets inside, it's dark, but that was no surprise to him; he already knew that mama lights were off. He doesn't have a flashlight, but he does have a cigarette lighter. He strikes it for light as he calls out in the dark house to the kids, but some are dead. The others were too afraid to answer him fearing that they would give away their hiding place. But then, Otis saw it. He saw all the blood. One of the policemen was hiding behind the door. Now, he has blocked the door and got his gun out telling Otis to get down on the floor. Otis knew that he planned to kill him. He saw and understood what they have already done to Tracy, plus it's a white man that he has never seen before and a cop. So Otis made a break for it, ran into Mama's room, and shut the door.

He is trying to block off the door with that brown file cabinet that was at the foot of Mama's bed. He grabs the iron crowbar to fight them off him, but by now, all of the policemen came out of hiding, and they really need to get to Otis because he is older and he is hollering louder. The other kids who are still in hiding heard all of this and were glad that they didn't answer Otis when he was calling out to them. All three of the policemen kicked the door to Mama's room at the same time, and the door just about came off the hinge. They muscled their way in on Otis, and he was swinging that crowbar hitting the white guy that gave them a ride and showed them the house in the head and killed him. Now the policemen are really mad, so they shot Otis point-blank in the head.

But now they got more problems. They got the secretary telling them that the mother and Eddie Giddy were back and would be coming home any minute now; plus they have a dead white man on their hands. Mama leaves the store and pulls up in front of the house. Mama saw what looks like a glimpse of light from a flashlight, and she noticed that none of the kids came to the window or the door even after Eddie was blowing his horn, so Mama told Vanessa to get out and take the toys she brought the kids from the auction in the house. Vanessa said she was scared because it was so dark, and there were no movements. She said, "Let's go down to granddad's and pick up the baby, and we all can come back and go in the house together." So Eddie took off, went down to my grandparent's, and dropped my aunt Charlotte off on the way. The police heard the truck when it pulled up, and they were prepared to kill each and every one who would come through the door. But then, they heard the truck took off and they knew that it was now or never, they were running out of time. They had a white body that they needed to get rid of, and they needed the rest of the kids dead, but didn't have time to look for them any longer. So they felt that the best thing to do at that point was to set the house on fire and try to burn up everything.

They went through the house dashing gas everywhere that they thought that the kids would be hiding. The white guys that were sent down to the house, by the secretary of the fire department, were to bring some gas to the police. This was so they could pour gas in different parts of the house. Once the cocktails were thrown, the house was to be engulfed in flames. The same guys were seen leaving the house running and jumping into a truck with squealing tires as they fled the scene.

The police figured that it would be better for them if they just hide out in that shed between our house and the house next door and just come out when the fire trucks and all the people shows up and just be another face in the crowd. So while Mama and them were at my grandparents' house to pick up the baby, Mama was also talking to her mother telling her all about the things that she had brought at the auction. It's only been about thirty minutes since they pulled away from in front of the house.

There was a knock at the door, and my aunt Darleen goes to the door and asks, "Who is it?" The police stated their identity and asked directly for Eddie. Neither he nor his parents lived there, so Darleen came back to her mother's room where everyone was sitting and talking at and told Eddie that the police was at the front door asking for him. He gets up and goes to the door, and as soon as they saw him, they told him that your house just blew up. Eddie replied, "That can't be, we just left from the house?" What Eddie didn't know was that Gina's boyfriend had just walked by the house not even five minutes ago and the only thing that he noticed was different was that there was no talking or laughing, like you would normally hear at night, especially since the utilities had been off.

He was walking by on his way to his mom's house that was only about five hundred yards away from my mother's house. And as soon as he walked in his mom's house, he went straight to the bathroom. As he took off his shirt, he heard a very loud explosion. He looked out the bathroom window and sees the fire, and realizes it's our house, so he puts back on his shirt. He left his mom's house, ran back over to our house as fast as he could, but he can't get in because of the fire that's at the front door, but he can go to the side of the house and break a window and yell into the house. And so he did, then he heard someone inside moaning. They were stilling alive, but they couldn't talk. They were clinging on for dear life. I can only imagine what thoughts going through their heads as they lay there dying. The only thing that he could think to do next was to come out to Jerry's café where Dwayne and I were at. I can remember it just like it was yesterday. Dwayne was the DJ, and I was sitting at a table when Martin Louis ran through the door and came to my table and told me that our house had just blown up. I wasn't sure that I heard him right the first time, and when I saw that he wasn't playing, I said what then he said to me, "Yawl house is on fire." I immediately ran up to the DJ stand and told Dwayne, and everybody in the café knew that something serious had happened by the way that we left. Dwayne had just up and left the DJ stand, and I followed behind him as fast as I could. Neither of us owned a car at the time, so we left running on foot. We could see the fire in the sky when we first step out of the café door. But for some reason, the fire looked further down from where our house was. Yet, the closer I got, the more I realized that it was, in fact, our house. When Dwayne and I got to the whites-only club that sit in the middle of town, we split up. I turned to the left, right beside it, but Dwayne kept going. He ran right past the front of it. There were some white guys standing out front, and when they saw Dwayne run past them, they started calling him all kinds on "n" words and racist names. Some of them started to run after him, so Dwayne stopped and picked up a handful of rocks and threw them at those guys who were chasing him to make them turn around. I don't think that they knew who we were or why we were running at the time. I think that they were just some white guys that had too much to drink and bored and wanted to do what they was used to doing when they have been drinking and that was to catch a black man by himself. They call that having fun, but we call it an act of terror because a black man running at night in the dirty south in a town where it was a known fact that whites had been killing blacks with a mob of white men chasing you is terrifying.

I made it to the house first. There was only one fire truck there and two firemen. I grabbed one of them by the arm and I asked him was anybody home? Because I had noticed that Eddie's truck was gone, but I also knew that someone was always up in our house as well. But deep down inside this was one time that I was hoping that the kids was with Mama, and with the truck being gone, I still had a little hope in spite of the fact that the fireman snatched his arm from me and said that he didn't know if anybody was home or not, but that if they were, they would be dead by now. They were not putting any water on the fire because they said that they ran out and left the tool that they needed to turn the water on with. So standing there, not knowing if anybody was in the house or not wasn't agonizing enough, but having to stand there with the fireman and watch and listen to the house just burn while nobody was doing anything was like something that you would see in a horror movie. By now, all of the neighbors are coming out in the streets, people from the north end of town and people from the south end. There were even people there from out of town, and some of them were saying that they were calling the fire department and someone just kept picking up the phone and hanging it back up.

A few minutes after I had gotten to the house, Dwayne arrived. I still had little hope that the kids were in the truck with Mama and them.

But then, Eddie's truck pulled up with a car right behind it, and before the car could come to a complete stop, Mama jumped out of the truck and started screaming, hollering, and crying. It was at that very moment that I knew that someone was definitely in that burning house. Crowds of people were gathering from everywhere, then we noticed three more white men coming out of that little shed that sited between our house and the house next door. They were wearing khaki outfits, and they all had guns in their hands. But we didn't recognize any of them. We were wondering who are all of these new faces? Then it dawned on us, this was in fact a hit on our family. It's the reason why the fire department was not taking the calls, and it's the reason why they are not fighting the fire. They are trying to let this house burn up. With nobody doing anything, Dwayne ran into the burning house and a few minutes later, he came out and said that he saw the kids bodies and that they were burning blue flames. Eddie and my uncles were trying to cut their way into Mama's room with the axe that we used to cut firewood with because we knew that's where the kids would be at. Finally, they started to put water on the house, then the policemen that we didn't know went to the Augusta police and were talking like they were whispering in their ears.

Unexpectedly, they dropped the fire hose on the ground and formed a football huddle. When they came out of the huddle, they came out with guns and ordered everybody to get back. They made Eddie and the rest put down the axe and get back, and then the order was given to shoot and kill any "n" word who would try to come back up to that house. So there we were, standing out in the middle of the street at gunpoint being called many kinds of the "n" word as they were swearing at us. By then, Dwayne had been in the house at least two more times. The last time he ran in the house, the police sprayed him in the face with some Mace as he was entering the house. When he got in there, he could not open his eyes to see his way back out, so Gina brother-in-law Lucas Louis, and Logan Jack's brother Nathan Brown went in after him as the police were beating them with their billy clubs to stop them. Dwayne was telling us that he had seen Otis in there also, and that he was standing up with his fist balled up dead.

They were making it very clear that they were trying to let the house burn all the way down with the kids in it to cover up the slaughter that they had done.

While we were all at gunpoint, it seemed as if time stood still. The house was burning and the kids were in it, and no one was doing anything about it. All of the firefighters were just standing around observing, Mama was begging and pleading with them to save her babies. Then one of the policemen who we didn't know said to the others that one of them got away and that he hid in one of the backrooms and Mama heard him say it, so she started telling them that all of the kids were in her room because she didn't realize that he was talking about what he knew from the time that he was in the house. So they grabbed the axe that they had made Eddie Giddy and the others put down and started to walk to the back of the house with it. Mama was starting to walk behind them telling them that the kids were in her room. I knew that they were going to finish the job, and if Mama followed them back there, they were going to kill her too and would've made up some kind of excuse why they had to do it.

I yelled to Mama and told her not to go back there with them, and she turned around. They went on around there with that axe, but when they came back, they didn't have the axe with them, and we never saw it again. Everything has been revealed; what they were doing was intentional. They did not even have an ambulance there. About four in the morning, the coroner's office came with a hearse to get the bodies. One by one they were bringing them out. Then we noticed that one of them is a big and long body which we automatically assumed was Choppy. I couldn't take it anymore so I left and went down to our grandparents' house. Those who stayed said that they counted at least six bodies; some said more. The police told everybody to go home, and that a fire marshal would be there at 9:00 a.m. to tell us what had happened but we already knew.

Eventually, those who stayed came down to our grandparents too. We were crying and in shock trying to make sense of it all.

Now the funeral home was owned by a father and son, but it was the son who came and picked up the bodies. He was also known among blacks as a member of the Ku Klux Klan. Around seven o'clock in the morning, it was the father who came knocking at my grandparent's door. He said that he needed to talk to my mother, but they didn't let him in yet because we didn't know just who we could trust. But he kept saying that he really needed to talk to my mother, so they let him in. I escorted him to the living room where we were all sitting. He asked my mother if he could have her permission to bury the kids today. My mother said, "No, my babies aren't even cold yet." They had only been dead for about six hours. Then he said, "Well, I want you to promise me that you or no one in your family will try to open them caskets. See, I can't say too much because I could end up with a bullet in my head." And then he left. About nine in the morning, we all left from my grandparents' and went back up to the house that burned. There was daylight now, and we could clearly see the magnitude of damage that was done to what was just a few days ago our home.

The Cover-Up

There were news reporters there from Little Rock and Memphis; they wanted to know how the fire started since there were no utilities on at the house. The news was there so fast they caught the officials off guard, and they didn't even have time to get their story straight. People were telling them about the explosion that they heard, and others were saying how that they were calling the fire department and could not get through. We were telling them that the Ku Klux Klan did it, and that the officials were a part of it, but it was just your word against theirs. We were hoping that the fire marshal would prove us right, but at nine o clock, he didn't show up. Then the police said that the fire marshal that was supposed to be there was not coming because he fell and broke his leg, but that another one would be coming. While the news reporters were there filming, my mother spotted some clothes in a basket that used to be in a closet before Captain Linden Dirk threw them out into the yard. They filmed my mother as she went under the tape and picked up a piece of clothing that was soaked in blood. Everybody knows that a burnt body doesn't bleed because the blood is consumed by the fire itself. Those clothes were kept in a closet so that meant that one of the kids was hiding there before they were shot or stabbed to death. We didn't know much about the law then, but we knew that he was tampering with evidence. And as you can see, the fire marshal has not arrived yet, but the police are in the house throwing stuff out in the yard, scraping stuff up off the floor, and putting some of it in piles already.

About noon, the fire marshal came and everybody was waiting to hear what his finding was going to be. Everybody was waiting on an answer, and I can remember thinking that this must be a very smart man. I mean, he must be extra smart because he don't have any tools of any kind, and if he could just look at this house and tell what happened here then he was going to be someone fascinating to watch. The truth of the matter is, he was a part of the chaos. He had gone to the Woodruff County Police Department before he came down to the house, and the police had already told him what they had done. So instead of him trying to find the real reason of what really happened, he would take on the role of a cleaner. He left the house, went back up to the jail, got an inmate out—a white guy by the name of Richard James, and they took him to his house for him to get his chainsaw. They went back to the house that burned, cut up the floors in the house around the space heaters then they walked around the house. When they got to the place where the gas meter was, before they pulled it, they found a piece of black rubber hose. It was as if they wanted Richard James to witness them finding it. The piece of hose had come off of an old Ranger-type washing machine. They needed an explanation fast due to all of the pressure from the media while the public was still waiting on an answer, while some were saying that it was an explosion. One man even told the reporter that he saw the fire started outside the house at the front door.

They needed a cause, and they needed one fast, so they made up one. Apparently, our family was accused of starting the fire by trying to hook that black piece of rubber hose up to the pipes where the meter once was before the light company came and took it away. If they would have stopped there, they might would have gotten away with that lie, but by them trying to explain it, they messed up and said that it was because of a leak in a gas line. That got the attention of the Arkansas pipeline commission, and before they could come down from Little Rock and do an investigation, the news media was already on ready, set, go. So they took the police and fire marshal's report about a leak in a gas line and ran with it. It was all over the news that a leak in a gas line was to blame.

Take a minute and use your imagination for a moment of review. My stepdad left us, we lost our brick home, and wore the embarrassment when we moved into an old house that needed lots of work. We lost that house that we were calling home along with all of our clothes and other stuff, we were basically homeless. We had five members of our family dead, and then they broadcasted our misfortunes all over the news. The word all around town was that we were stealing gas, blown our house up, and killed the kids. I still cry sometimes when I think about it. All that had happen was that the news had bounced all over it so fast until the officials didn't have time to get their story together so they put the blame on the ones that had already lost everything. Eventually, the Arkansas pipeline commission came and did their investigation, and their finding was that there was no way that the piece of black rubber hose could have fit those gas meter pipes and that the pipes still had the packing down in them. So when the fire marshal saw that he couldn't get away with a leak in a gas line, he made one more attempt to get the officials off the hook. He would say that he don't know how the fire started, but that it started at an overstuffed chair in the living room. A chair that the police threw out into the front yard before the fire marshal arrived, so the fire marshal ruled the fire accidental because if it is an accident then there is no killer on the loose, and if there is no killer on the loose then there is no need to further investigate.

We didn't have any burial insurance, so some of the people in Augusta set up a burial fund for us at the Bank of Augusta, which I thought was a very nice thing to do. I only wish that they would have come together like that and help Mama with those light bills. About four or five days after the fire, we were over to my aunt's house—you know, the bebes— and the same white guy Richard James who the fire marshal had gotten out of jail came over. His mother lived only two houses down from my aunt's house. They had lived there for years so we knew him for years. We used to play together as kids. They were one of the few families who weren't racist although some of their relatives were members of the Ku Klux Klan. As a matter of the fact, his brother and I were classmates; we even went to the *Bozo Show* together in the third grade in which they still have a picture of that on their wall. He was crying and telling us how sorry he was for our loss. But then he started saying things that were almost unbelievable, but it confirmed just what we had already known.

He started by saying that while he was still in jail, Captain Linden Dirk took him out of jail, took him down to the house, and asked him if he had ever seen a body burned blue flames. This happened the night of the fire, before the police even came down to my grandparents' looking for Eddie Giddy to tell him that his house has just blown up. He went on to say that it in fact it was the Ku Klux Klan that killed the kids and that Otis had put up a good fight. He asked me if I had noticed the hinges that was on Mama's bedroom door. He said that there were too many and that they were too big for Otis. Otis had used that brown file cabinet that was at the foot of Mama's bed to block the door and to keep them out. The reason that the hinges was almost out was because they were kicking the door down. He said that Otis was using that steel crowbar that Eddie used to use to stir the ashes with to fight them off until they killed him by shooting him almost point blank in the head.

He turned to Eddie and said, "They were looking for you, Eddie. They asked a smooth-faced black guy if you were home, and he must've said yes."

At that point, we knew that it must to have been Logan Jack Brown because he was in his thirties and could not grow a beard. He proceeded to tell Eddie that they had a meeting at the whites-only club. Now I'm thinking that maybe those white guys who were chasing Dwayne did know where and why we were running. He said, "They all had agreed to kill you, Eddie, but when they had gotten in the house, they realized that it were only the kids in there, so they killed them to keep them from identifying them. Now at this time, all the kids' bodies were in Little Rock at the state medical crime lab for autopsy. I was led to believe that Richard James must have been in that house before it burned because of the fact that he had said that Otis used that brown file cabinet that was at the foot of Mama's bed to block the door with it. Well, Richard James had never been in our house before, so how did he know where the file cabinet used to be, and how did he know that the file cabinet was brown when in fact after the fire, the cabinet was burn to a crisp with no color on it at all, and it was one of the thing that the police had thrown out in the yard before the fire marshal got there. But Richard James said, "They're going to tell you all that all of the kids died from smoke inhalation, and that they were paying the state medical examiner fifteen thousand dollars to falsify the autopsy reports. Richard James said that the reason why he knows what they were going to say was because he was riding in the car with Officer Linden Dirk when it came over the police scanner that that's what they were going to say. Now that we knew just what they were going to say, we knew that we was going to need some help, so I called CNN. They told me to go and get a copy of the police and fire department report and send it to them, but they also advised me that if they would give me a hard time to just leave it and don't worry about it and that they would get it. I got my cousin Leon, who was my uncle Johnny's oldest son, who we had nicknamed Boomer, to go with me to ask for them, and I decided to go to the fire department first, but not to the actual fire station because Augusta only had a volunteer fire department, so they didn't have people at the station at all times. But everybody knew that the secretary of the fire department worked at the same store that Mama and they had stopped at that night to buy batteries; it is also the same store that they got their gas from to burn the house down with, so we went there first.

When Boomer and I walked in, I went straight to him and said, "I would like a copy of the fire department report." The volunteer bucked his eyes as if he was surprised. He started walking toward the back of the store, so we followed him thinking that he was going to get the copy of the fire report, but about halfway through the store sit a desk with a scanner on it. He pulled out a drawer, and instead of giving us a copy of the fire report, he pulled out a copy of an autopsy report of my little sister Tracy, but the kids' bodies were still in Little Rock at the crime lab. It was as if the state medical examiner had sent them that copy to say this is what they are going to look like. And then he started saying stuff like, "This is bigger than what y'all think it is," and, "Y'all need to just leave it alone."

So I said to him, "You're right, it's bigger than what you think it is."

He replied by mentioning that there is a lot of paperwork to make a fire report, "It's a long sheet of paper."

Then I said to him, "You're the secretary of the fire department, there's been a fire and five kids are dead, and you don't have a fire report?

But you have an autopsy report of a little dead black girl that you don't even know."

Then someone started to talk over the scanner saying its two of them going around asking for some copies of a report. Whoever was on the other end asked, "Who sent them clowns up there?"

They said, "I don't know, and do you want us to pick them up?" The other person said no.

Then I said to the secretary, "These are your friends who are calling us names, and talking about us like that. Do you think that's right for them to be talking about us like that?"

He answered me no with a look on his face, as if he were wishing they would shut up because the people they were talking about were right there listening. It was the police we're talking about picking us up, so I knew that we were not going up to the police station to ask for anything. I called CNN again and told them what had happened, and they were like, "Okay, don't worry about it, we'll get it."

After a few days, I stopped at that store to get some gas. When I went in to pay, I put my money on the counter, instead of him taking the money, he reached out a long sheet of paper to me and said, "This is what you asked me for. It was just a sheet of paper from a photocopier. Instead of being an 8-1/2 × 11, it was an 11 × 14, and it only had writing on one side that said: "Cause of fire: Leaking gas line." A few more days went by, Richard James, who told us that the Klan killed the kids, came back and said that the kids' bodies were back from Little Rock. So just like the last time, we all went up to the funeral home, and just as he had said, the bodies were back and the funeral director handed us a piece of paper that stated all of the kids died of smoke inhalation just as he said that they were going to say. Then they commenced to say that when they were going to put the kids in the ground, mind you, we were not allowed to see the kids at all; not even my mother to identify them, plain and simple. The last time that any of us had seen the kids was when they were alive. Now Mama had a cousin who lived in Saint Louis. He owned a funeral home, and he wanted to donate some caskets to help out with funeral expenses. But the white owner of the funeral home in Augusta said that no other funeral homes can come in and provide any kinds of services but that we had to purchase the caskets from him. They didn't want to have the funeral on the inside of the church because they anticipated a large crowd. It was going to be a graveside funeral.

On the day of the funeral, it was as if the police were preparing to kill again. We were all meeting up at my grandparents. *We* , meaning everybody. People were there from different parts of Arkansas to pay their respects, while the police were using intimidation tactics. They kept passing by riding four deep and showing off their shotguns. They had already asked my mother to promise that none of us would try to open any of those caskets. They were anticipating some retaliation from us. Then they pulled a fast one on us. They told us that the funeral would start at a certain time, but they went ahead and put the boxes down in the ground with the caskets before we arrived at the gravesite. By doing it that way, they were making sure that none of us would try to open those caskets. So we really don't know if anything is in those caskets or not, but then again one of theirs could be buried down there with those kids. The way I see it is that there had to be a reason why they made us promise not to open any of those caskets. When we did get a chance to walk through the house, we found a cap and a pair of sunglasses in Mama's room on the countertop. We knew they didn't belong to any of us. It was the kind of sunglasses that a white boy would wear and the cap had something about Budweiser on it, and it was not burn although everything else was burned up. And with everybody saying that they counted six bodies instead of five, we were led to believe that maybe Otis killed one of them, and maybe that's who that cap and glasses belonged to. And with the media all over the case, they knew that they could not afford to have a funeral of a white man during the same time as ours. So they very well may have buried him with the kids and that might help explain why they wanted us to promise, after the kids had only been dead for six hours, that none of us would try to open any of those caskets. We were told that four hundred and some peoples showed up at that graveside funeral. I don't think that anybody really knew how many people were there, but it was a lot and it was by far the largest funeral that's ever been in Augusta especially among blacks until this day.

Aftermath

After the funeral, we were still living with reality here and there. I would go to church and hang out with my best friend Willie, and he would be doing the best that he could to comfort me. We started to walk the streets again at night talking, but this time only back and forth between his and my grandparents' house. And even though things where bad, we would still fantasize about having a good life. One night, it was Willie, Boomer, and I walking and fantasizing. We said that Willie and I would marry two sisters, and that Boomer would marry their niece. I said that I would one day live in New York and that we were going to be rich. Well, ain't nothing wrong with a little daydreaming. I have found it to be a temporary way to escape a harsh reality. We didn't want to live in Woodruff County anymore because we weren't sure if they were planning to come back and kill the rest of us or what. Plus, Richard James had told Eddie Giddy that they wanted him bad, real bad. Eddie knew that living in Augusta, Woodruff County, was no longer safe for him. Eventually we moved to Newport, Arkansas. Eddie's parents lived there. It was about thirty-five miles north of Augusta. It was the town that Mama told the kids that she was going to move to. If those race-haters would have waited just one more day, Mama could have moved and maybe those kids would still be alive today. It was a long desolated highway between Newport and Augusta, and whenever we would go back to visit our relatives, we would be sure to leave before nightfall, and even though we had our own house and didn't have to live on kinfolks without the kids being there it just wasn't the same.

We were hurt and starting all over again. It was like a nightmare that you couldn't wake up from. The look in my mother's eyes was a look of despair. All she could think of both night and day was what could she had done differently that would have not allowed her to be in this situation. We wanted revenge, and I will be the first to tell you that I had lots of evil thoughts. I was a military man; I knew how to kill, and there were times when I felt like going to all the houses of those who were involved, knock on the door, and kill whoever answered it. But then I also knew that, that would make me no better than them—a murderer, and the thought of me being the same as them made me sick to my stomach.

A lawyer out of Little Rock whose name was Samuel E. Wright heard about the tragedy and saw it on the news. He knew that we didn't have any money yet and still he asked my mother if he could take the case with the understanding that we would give him whatever money we could put together from time to time to help out with some of the case expenses. It was our chance to get revenge and a way that nobody had to die, so my mother told the lawyer yes. At first, he was not sure which way to go with it.

He wanted to go have a criminal investigation and try to find the murderers, which were going to be very hard to do without any money. And when we, the family, started to ask people in the neighborhood what they knew about the tragedy, they made it very clear to us real fast that they didn't want anything to do with the case. Because blacks had been killed before and nothing was done about it, and they still wanted to live. When we told this to the attorney, he decided to go civil first and try to get some money so that we would later be able to fight for a criminal investigation and to try and get those kids bodies up. So he filed a civil lawsuit in the amount of ten million dollars against the city of Augusta, Arkansas, in Woodruff County; five million dollars against the Augusta Police Department; and five million dollars against the Augusta Fire Department. I can still remember the first time that I heard it in the news on the radio and how I felt that they were finally going to pay for what they did. But in actuality, it was going to be a long, painful, agonizing five years before the case would even go to trial. In any case, the announcement went out over the radio the same day that the lawsuit was filed. And when the blacks in town heard about it, they started to look at us dramatically different. There were some that thought we had the nerves of steel, and that we should have just let it go and not try to stand up and fight the white folks because that's what the blacks in Woodruff County was accustomed to. But there were others that saw us as some heroes, and said that it was about time that somebody black stood up to the white folks. So you could tell that things must have been real bad between the black and the white folks, when just the filing of a lawsuit was counted as a victory even before it went to trial.

Contrary to their popular opinion, they both were right, it took some nerves to stand up to some white people whom you know would kill you for doing it. But I had been taught all of my life that I was no better than anyone else and that no one was any better than me. I read a license plate once that said: Give Me Liberty or Give Me Death. So at that point, it no longer matter what people thought about us. More importantly, we knew that it was the right thing to do and so we did. I was the spokesperson for my family when it came to dealing with the media. And because I would be on television in the news, it made them hate me even the more. So because I drove back and forth from Newport to Augusta on that long desolated highway, my family feared for my life. One day, my grandfather called me to him and gave me a snub-nosed .32 pistol. He said, "Just in case they would try to catch me on that highway by myself to kill me then I would have something to defend myself with." The old folks used to say that "when it rains, it pours."

My marriage after six years ended in a divorce. My wife took my son and left me and moved back to Saint Louis. I can remember feeling like my whole world was falling apart and that everything that could go wrong did go wrong. I started to date a good-looking young lady whose name was Velma Houston out of Newport, Arkansas. Unfortunately, because I had just lost my first wife, I really wasn't sure what direction I wanted to go in within our relationship.

One day, I went down to Cotton Plant, and on my way down, I stopped in Gregory and picked up my cousin Ethan, Boomer's brother, and had him to ride to Cotton Plant with me. On the way back, my car started to run hot. It was on a hot summer day, and we were on a long desolated highway as well, kind of like the one between Newport and Augusta. So I slowed down, and we finally came to some houses. So we stop at the first set of houses that we came to, I got out of the car, went up on the porch, and knocked on the door. A white guy came to the door, and just by the way that he looked at me when he opened the door, I could hear it in his voice that he didn't like blacks. At that point, I really didn't want to ask him for anything, but I definitely didn't want to blow my car engine either. It was already evening, and I didn't want to be there by nightfall. You talking about an awkward moment. He didn't want to give me anything, but he also didn't want me broke down right in front of his house. I, on the other hand, didn't want to have to ask him for anything, but I didn't want to be stranded right in front of a race-hater's house so he closed the door. A few minutes later, he opened it with some water. It wasn't much but it was enough for us to cool the engine down. I wasn't going to ask him for more, and I wasn't going to stay there, so we took our time and made it to the town of Gregory. We still needed more water, so Ethan had me to stop at some of his friend's house, who just happens to be white. After all, Ethan lived in Gregory, and his daddy worked for the Cesars' farm.

While I was under the hood of my car filling my radiator with the water that they had given me, out of the house comes a very beautiful young lady, who walked right up to me intently and immediately started talking to me. She told me her name was Juliette, and that she was from Oklahoma. I started to look around to see if Ethan and his friends were playing a joke on me or what.

I could not believe it. I mean that kind of stuff just don't happen in that day; not in that part of Arkansas. The only way that a black man could date a white woman and get away with it, and I mean no disrespect, was only if she was fat and ugly, but this girl was mixed white and American Indian. She was very beautiful. We talked for a while, but it was getting dark, and I still had to go through Augusta to go home in Newport. When you leave Augusta going to Newport, the first curve that you come to is called Negro Head Corner. Legend has it, years ago, the Ku Klux Klan would nail black men to a big old tree by their ear and then take a whip and beat them until they pulled themselves off the tree. Then they would hang them. The Klan members used to have a wooden head of a black man on a steak and that's how it got its name. Needless to say, I didn't want to be caught anywhere near Augusta at nightfall anymore.

I had left Augusta late one night. As I came into the small community of Tupelo, Arkansas, my car threw a rod through the engine, and I was sixteen miles from Newport and thirteen miles back to Augusta. I knew that if I would've tried to walk back to Augusta and if some of those white race-haters would see me. I wouldn't be here to talk about it today, so I took my chances and walked those sixteen miles to Newport, down a long, deserted, and very dark highway that didn't have streetlights. While I was walking, a truck came from the town of Patterson Way, and as it passed me by, they yelled out the "n" word and although they didn't offer me a ride, deep down inside I knew that I was better off than to try to walk back to Augusta because they, meaning the people in the passing truck, didn't recognize me as the spokesperson for my family and didn't want to kill me. They were just doing what they considered to be fun.

Juliette and I had exchanged phone numbers before I had left. So I was calling her, and she was calling me; and because I lived so far away, I would go down to visit her only on weekends at first. But the more we talked, the more interested I became to her. She had been raised up from a child being told to never date a black man because they stink, steal, and don't work, yet she was still interested in me. She had never listened to rap or any black music before, and to me that was a challenge. I was determined to change all of that. So we kept calling each other. Like clockwork, I would go and see her every weekend. It was official, we were dating, and we eventually fell in love. Instead of me waiting until the weekend to go, I started going during the week to see her, because she would call me and tell me to come. But there was just one small problem, I got this beautiful girl in Newport whose name was Velma that I was dating also. So I said to myself, *I'll keep them both because they live so far apart they'd never find out about one another.* The word had gotten out in Augusta among the blacks that a white girl and I were dating. We both knew what could happen to me if the wrong race-haters found out about it. We both wanted to be together, but not at the expense of the other one's life. I had a cousin who was living in New York. We were talking about moving there. We had been talking on the phone, and I told her that I was going to be coming down so that we could hang out like normal times, and of course, she was saying that she can't wait to see me and how much she missed me and stuff like that.

It was Halloween night. I was going to stay all night and leave the next day. This was October 31, 1987. I must have made it to her house around ten o'clock, and of course, by now all the white guys who were Ethan's friends were my friends too. They knew that Juliette and I were dating and they didn't have a problem with it. As a matter of fact, if I drank too much or if it got too late then they would insist that I spend the night, so when I arrived, they were glad to see me as well then one of them went in the house and told Juliette that I was outside. But she sent him back out telling me that she was not finished getting dress yet and for him to tell me to go to town and go to the liquor store before it closed. She would be ready by the time I got back. I left and went to the liquor store, got what we were going to be drinking, and came back. Instead of stopping at her house, I went another six or seven miles down past her house to the graveyard where the kids were buried. I was drinking and thinking, I knew that if they would have still been alive, they would have been trick or treating; after all, they were just kids and it was Halloween night.

Finally, I left and went back to Juliette's house to pick her up and as long as I had been gone, I figured she had to have gotten dress by now. So I pulled up, parked, got out of my car, and leaned up against the trunk of my car talking to the guys that I had met through Ethan. But then the next thing that I knew, I woke up on the ground sitting up against the door of my car. What was so bad about it was I didn't know why or what had happened. All I know was that I was cold and my head was hurting. When I touched the top of my head with my fingertips of my right hand and looked at it, I saw blood but I still didn't know what had happened. I was lost. I looked at my watch and it was about forty-five minutes that I couldn't give an account for. I could see people walking with their children, but no one was saying anything to me so I got up, got in my car, and went down to my uncle Johnny's house. I asked my cousin Ethan have he been out to the store tonight, and before he could answer me, I noticed that he was not even dressed yet. He replied no, and about that time, my memory started to come back. Having a flashback, I saw this white face. As he clenched his fist onto my clothes in my chest area, he was shaking me as he was saying to me, "You remember this face, boy."

And then it hit me, this white boy had jumped on me, and I didn't even know the reason why. But one thing that I did know was that he had messed with the wrong one, baby, my family was dead, and I had just left their graves. I had lost my wife, I had been drinking, and I had a gun. I was a walking time bomb. I had had it up to my forehead with this "I'm better than you" attitude. I wasn't taking it anymore. So I left out of my uncle's house, got in my car, and down that gravel road I went as fast as I could without having a wreck. When I got back to the place where I had got jumped at, I started to look for that face that I saw in that flashback. It was a group of white people huddled up about fifty yards from me and then I saw the silhouette of the face that I didn't know but had seen in a flashback, so I got my pistol in my hand and opened my car door. I got out with the pistol behind my back and with my left foot on the ground and my fight foot on the floorboard, I yelled out to him and asked him, "Why did you hit me? What did I ever do to you? I don't even know you." At that time, if he would have just said "I'm sorry, man," or something like that I would have just let it go, but he start saying stuff like "by God" this and that, and as far as I was concerned that was the wrong answer. So out with the pistol I came. Someone yelled, "He's got a gun" and people started to scream and run everywhere. In just an instance, all of the "I'm better than you" and "I am superior than you" became human. They were running for their lives. He started yelling that he had a gun also, and he started toward his truck. In Arkansas, you could have a gun rack in the back window of your truck, and it was not uncommon to see two or three rifles in the back window of a truck. But I was about to faint. I had gotten too mad too fast, my blood had gone to my head alone with that lick on the head. I was passing out while he was getting his gun to shoot me.

I was passing out and there was nothing I could do about it. I was shaking my head trying to regain consciousness. There was a black girl there named Emma Lakes. I asked her if she would start my car and drive it out of there with me hiding on the other side before I pass out and he end up shooting me point blank. But about that time, I could hear the police sirens. When I looked, it looked like *Smokey and the Bandit.* There were seven or eight police cars coming, and they all had their sirens and their lights on, so I took the bullets out of the gun and put it in my car. I put the gun in one place and the bullets in another and covered them with some newspapers and walked away from my car, so that the police would not have a reason to search my car. Plus I was still about to faint so as I was walking, I was shaking my head trying to keep from passing out. The next thing I knew I was on the ground with some big white cop on top of me putting some handcuffs on me. I already knew that this was going to be bad because I was the spokesperson for my family, and we already had a five-million dollar lawsuit pending against the city of Augusta Police Department and a five-million-dollar lawsuit against the Fire Department, which was in Woodruff County. They got me up off the ground and by then, a lot of white people had gather around. The only black people that were there was Emma Lakes and me, and the police told them that they were going to take me to jail. Right in my face, they told the white guy that had hit me to take his gun and go home. The little old white lady that ran the post offices, whose name was Mrs. Sophie Anderson, had gone into my car, found my pistol, put the bullets back in it, and gave it to the police just before they took me off to jail. I can remember thinking while I was in the backseat of that police car on my way back to the Woodruff County jail that I would be blessed if they really took me to jail and not take me off somewhere in the woods and kill me. That which was supposed to have been a great night for my girl and me turned out to be a nightmare. My head was hurting and all I could smell was blood. I smelled blood all night, and although they knew that the white boy had hit me in the head with something, they didn't offer me any medical attention. That night creeped by so slow, and the longer I sat there, the more that reality sunk in. Everything was about to come out, my girl in Newport was about to find out about the white girl plus I were going to need money to bail out, and because they had impounded my car, I was going to need money for that as well. I wanted to bail out fast, not just to get out of jail, but just in case they hadn't recognize who I was yet. I can remember thinking about how bad I had messed up. Our lawyer had already told us to be careful and not to get into any trouble as long as the lawsuit was pending because they would try to use it against us in court, but now my family was about to hear that I was in jail so it was very hard for me to sleep that night. It seemed as if morning was never going to come. I knew that once they realized who I was they were going to throw the book at me and try to charge me with the maximum. When morning came, that's exactly what they did. They gave me so many tickets they had to staple them together and looked like a little book. Word got out that I had been arrested and somehow Velma Houston, the young lady that I was dating in Newport, heard about it and came to bail me out. But as you know that came with a price; she had heard about the white girl too. I had some haters before the word was even popular, and even though she was letting me have it, I was still glad to see her and be out of jail. I found out from my best friend's older brother that they already knew who I was because he had heard it when it came over the scanner. That would explain why so many policemen came in the first place, that and the fact that I had a gun. After a few days, I went back to Gregory to see the white girl and the guys that I had been hanging out with to find out just what had happen. They began to tell me that when that one guy went in the house to tell Juliette that I was outside that the white boy named Billy Earl was in there. He had heard what the guy told Juliette and when he found out that Juliette and I were dating and that I was outside to pick her up, he went into a rage. Because he hated blacks and the thought of me being with a pretty white girl just drove him crazy.

He didn't stay there but had come up from what was known as the bottoms with his kids to take them trick or treating; instead he came outside and acted out his rage; without warning, he hit me over the head. Mama had always told us to be very careful dealing with them white girls because they would act like they care about you until trouble come and then they will yell "rape." That's what came to mind as Juliette was telling me that the same policeman whose name was Officer Clefus Kassie who threw me to the ground asked her to testify in court that she saw me pull the pistol and pulled the trigger and that she heard it snap because one of the bullets had a dent in it from the firing pin and they wanted to charge me with attempted murder. I then asked her if she was going to do it, and she said no because she loved me. She said that the same policeman asked her if she and I was having sex and that out of fear she told him no and then he said to her, "Good because if I would've caught you and him in the woods, I would've killed the both of you," but then officer Clefus Kassie turned right around and asked her if she would go out with him. She said that she told him no. One would think that after all that I had been through that the Augusta Police Department and their court system would have taken that in consideration and show me some mercy. I was out on bail, and I had to explain to my mother and the rest of them what had happened; how he had hit me in the head, but that I was the one that the police had taken to jail. When my court date came, I went and they postponed it. On the second court date, they gave me the name of a court-appointed attorney whose name was Bello A. Stone, and postponed it again. But this time, when I walked out of the courtroom, the same policeman who had thrown me to the ground and had said all of that to the white girl Juliette followed me out and came up to me with a piece of paper in his hand. As he reached it to me, I asked him what it was as I was opening it. They were charging me with assault in the first-degree. Since they could not get Juliette the white girl to testify against me, so they charged me with the next thing to it. On the third time that I went to court, the court-appointed lawyer, Mr. Bello A. Stone, didn't even show up. I had already been told that the lawyer that they had given me, Mr. Stone, had been busted for some marijuana on his own. The last man that he had represented was sent to prison for shoplifting and stealing some pork chops out of that same store that the secretary of the fire department worked at. This happened to be the same store that my mother had stopped at the same night that the kids were murdered in. This is where Boomer and I went to get a copy of the fire report while they called us names over the police scanner. So I knew that this was going to be real bad for me because if he had let a man go to prison for stealing some pork chops then I know that I didn't stand a chance. They were charging me with trying to kill a white man in the south. On the fourth time that I went to court, I met my so-called "lawyer," and he was looking like he was stoned, but he asked the court for more time so that he could prepare for the case. It was a rule that if a case went to trial five times and was not tried then it was to be thrown out, and I had gone four times already. Now on the fifth time that I went to court, I noticed that my lawyer was not there. The judge knew in fact that it was my fifth time also so I was kind of happy because I knew that they were supposed to throw it out, but instead the judge looked at me and said, "I don't care if your lawyer didn't show up, you're going to get some jail time." So they tried me without a lawyer, and I had to represent myself. White boy Billy Earl that had hit me was sitting on the front seat. They called me to the stand and then had me to raise my right hand and swear to tell the truth, but all the while I am thinking, *How dirty can these people be?* The reason that we are even here is because of their wickedness; this should be the other way around. I should be sitting on the front seat and the white boy Billy Earl should be on the stand. But after that I had raised my right hand and said that I will tell the truth, they started to say that I tried to kill the white boy with that gun and stuff like that; of course I denied it. I looked at the white boy, and he had a half smirk on his face as if he was really enjoying this, so I asked the court to let us go outside to settle this. If I win, I walk away with all charges dropped, but if I lose then the charges stick as they are. Judge Oliver said we can't do that so let's get on with the trial. Then the little old white lady Sophie Anderson, who ran the Gregory post office, testified against me. She was the one that had gotten in my car, got my pistol, put the bullets back in it, and gave it to the police. She told the court that she saw me pull the gun and that she heard me say that I would kill Billy Earl. I said to her, "If you were such a good person and you were for the right and justice then tell me why didn't you call the police when Billy Earl had hit me over the head with something and while I was unconscious, why didn't you call them while I laid out there on that cold ground for forty- five minutes to a half hour?" Sophie didn't reply, but the white boy burst out in court. I didn't use anything but my hands and instead of the judge using that outburst as evidence that Billy Earl had indeed assaulted me, they just giggled instead. I beat the resisting arrest charge because after Clefus Kassie testified, I asked him, "Did I tell you that I wasn't going with you?" and he answered no then I asked him did I try to fight you or anything and then he said no and that it was best that I didn't try to resist. He was being Mr. Tough Guy, but I proved my point, but yet and still he told the court how that he had hit me and threw me to the ground, and again they giggled. They were seeking to destroy my life, but God blessed me to slip right through their hands that day because even without a lawyer, I got the resisting arrest charge dropped and the assault in the first degree down to an assault in the third degree. Thank God that my lawyer didn't show up because he would have done more damage than good.

The judge still sentenced me to thirty days in the Woodruff County Jail. My family was dead and a ten-million dollar lawsuit was pending against the Augusta Police and Fire Department, I was the spokesperson on behalf of my family to the media, and now I have been hit over the head by a race-hater while he was being told to take his gun and go home to his family. I am going to jail and being charged with assault in the third degree. Surely you can understand why my family and I were a little afraid for me to be in that jail and in their custody. So much so until different family members were taking turns riding pass the jail to make sure that they were not going to try to take me out in the middle of the night and kill me. They also kept track of who the officers were on duty. My best friend Willie had already warn me not to take a trustee position. They had locked me up in the part of the jail that was under the ground, and believe it or not, I felt safer there than to be walking around freely because they could have shot and killed me, then lie and say that I was trying to escape. I can remember thinking a many late nights that when I would hear those jail doors open and slam that they might be coming for me to take me out in the cover of night to kill me. It was the first time that I had ever spent any real time in jail before, and as far as I was concerned, if I would live to make it out alive, it was going to be my last time too. Mama had raised us to stay away from people who stayed in trouble with the law; that also meant that I didn't hang with the people who were already locked up either when I got to jail. So I just prepared to be lonely in jail, until one day I heard the jail doors opened and slammed, and I saw this white man coming straight to my cell. It was my neighbor, Mason Carter, and just like everybody else whom we loved, we had given him a nickname also; we called him Red. They were putting him in my cell. It was a face that I knew and remembered from the better times of my life. Like when we were living in our brick house next door to Red. Daddy was home, and the kids were still alive, and Red had spent a many nights over to our house telling us all about his life back in Chicago. Red had a drinking problem, and that was why he was in jail. The Augusta Police had picked him up, arrested him, and charged him with public drinking. As soon as the police put him in the cell, Red told them that he had the shakes, so the chief of police Amando Dipak came back to the jail cell and brought him a cup of whiskey and passed it to him through the jail bars. And who would have ever thought that you could be put in a situation that just seeing the face of who was considered to be the town drunk could make your day. It amazed me how some people look down on people like Red, but I have been out in public and have seen a lady with a baby, and I have seen people go up to her even though they didn't knew her or the baby and would go as far as to play with and even kiss the baby, but then they are so soon to forget that people like Red was once somebody's baby. Shortly, after Red got out of jail, they sent him to the veterans hospital in North Little Rock, and because Augusta was so faraway, the veterans administration got Red an apartment right there in North Little Rock. I did twenty-two of the thirty days that they gave me then they let me out on good behavior and told me that if I did anything else that they would add those eight days to whatever new charges that I might get. As soon as I got out of jail, they made Billy Earl a trustee, and a few months later, they made him a police; yes you read it right the first time. He had gone from a tractor driver down in the bottoms to a police officer in Woodruff County. And as time went on, I moved to Little Rock, which was right across the river from Red, and so we stayed in touch with each other. Sometimes I would go pick him up and bring him over to have supper with me and my wife and kids. We would often talk about the time that we spent together in jail and reminisce about the time that we lived in

Woodruff County. I would often go by his apartment just to check on him to see how he was doing. One day, just like normal times, I went by his apartment to check on him, and as I was knocking on his door, his neighbor opened his door and stuck his head out and said that Red had gotten sick and that he had gone back to the veterans hospital. But this time, Red would not make it back out alive. I know to some he was just a town drunk, but to me and my family, he was a friend.

I don't walk around with a sign on my back saying that I am a victim of a group of race-haters which means that out of all that I have been through, I still encounter racists. I know the reason for one is that they don't know what I have been through already, or if they just don't like blacks then they don't care what you might have been through already. Maybe it's because I am not in the spotlight like some of the well-known civil rights activist, not that I am saying that they don't have to deal with it also, but maybe not as much as they would have to deal with it if they were not so well known. As soon as they made that white boy a police, he didn't waste any time showing the blacks in that town that he didn't care for blacks at all. He was stopping and harassing almost everyone who was black and driving. But whenever an opportunity came for him to help the blacks, he would act like he didn't want anything to do with it. I said that because a few months earlier, I went over to my Aunt Charlotte's house—you know the bebes—and she was telling me that her daughter Lesley had disciplined her daughter Latoya, which was my aunt's granddaughter, and that Latoya had ran away and had not come home in seven or eight hours, which was unusual for her to do. And that she was worrying about her, some of the family members were saying stuff like "don't worry, she'll be back" or "maybe she's over to a friend's house" or "don't worry, she's all right" and stuff like that. But then two days went by and there was still no Latoya and some of the police were helping to look for her; but not Billy Earl, he wouldn't help, and the others only helped for about three to four days. And after the police had stopped looking for her, we, the family and friends, had kept on looking. By now, twelve days had gone by and still no Latoya. We would spread out walking and calling out her name real loud. We must have searched that little town from top to bottom. After we had looked over the whole town, some said that they saw her go into the woods, so we started to search the woods. That led to the White River, and sure enough, we saw her footprints. We followed them all the way to the White River. There was only half of the last footprint because the water was washing it up on the bank of the river; and about five yards off of the bank in the water was a little tree branch and on it was Latoya's under slip and her dress and coat. By now, she had been missing for about twenty days; and there were rumors that a little white girl at school was saying that her daddy have Latoya in there basement. In all, Latoya had been missing for twenty-five days before some white man who was supposed to had been fishing found her body in the White River and called the police. She was found eight miles against the flow of the river and from where we found her footprints and clothing. Her footprints indicated that she may have been picked up by someone with a small boat. Her autopsy report said that she was in the water for twelve days, so we would often wonder who had her and where was she for the other thirteen days. There was no arrest, nobody spent one night in jail for it, and what few police did get involved barely helped us look for her, less known look for a murderer. Not long after that, my aunt Charlotte got a phone call. It was the voice of a white person. They told her to get her mother, which was my great-grandmother, and get out of that house because "they" meaning the race-haters were going to do to you the same thing that they had done to that girl on Fifth Street, referring to my mother, and talking about the house that was at 505 South Fifth Street where the kids got murdered. So my aunt called the police and the sheriff—I mean the head sheriff—Roscoe Dillon, himself came down to my aunt's house. I was over there when he walked through the door. She began to tell him about the threatening phone call that she received, and he told her that he knew about it already, and that she didn't have anything to worry because he has already talked to them boys about that. Then he went out to the police car, popped his trunk, got a hog's head out that they had butchered, carried it into the house, and gave it to my aunt. He asked her to vote for him and to ask everybody in the church to vote for him, but we were not taking any chances, so we got every gun that we could find and hid in the trees. There was a big ditch that ran along the south side of my aunt's house, and some of us were down in it with guns just waiting on some white person to come there and to try to do anything. We were going to kill them or they were going to have to kill us, but either way we had had it, enough was enough. My family was dead, and Latoya was dead; her autopsy said that she died on February 23, 1986. God blessed us that night because during that time in Augusta, it was common to see a truckful of white boys riding around in their four-wheel drive that would be covered with mud; and if you were black and walking, they would pass by and call you all kinds of racist names such as cs and monkeys pouch, just all kinds of racist names. I said that God blessed us, but the truth of the matter is God blessed them too. Because as trigger happy as we were that night, there was no doubt in the back of my minds that if a truckful of white boys would have drove by, somebody would have died; the sad part about it is they may not have known anything about a threatening phone call. Every time I think about that night, I can't help but thank God that no truckful of white boys passed by. Black people were being killed, and nothing was being done about it. A car own by a black man, whose name was Edwin John, was found off the road pushed up in some bushes on the outskirt of town, but he could not be found; he was missing for a week before his body was found across a field standing up in a slough dead. And nobody spent a night in jail for it; just the black folks talking among themselves. After a few days had gone by, another black man by the name of Morgan Bell was found dead. This time right outside of his home; he was beaten to death. The blacks in town were saying that a white man offered to buy his land that he lived on partly because it was on the outskirt of town and that it had two private fishponds on it, but he refused to sell it. Because the house that he lived in was kind of old, it didn't have a breaker box inside of the house, but had a fuse box outside the house. So the word was among the blacks that the white man went there and messed with the fuse box that made the lights go out, and so naturally Mr. Bell went outside thinking that he had blown a fuse only to be beaten to death and that's where they found him at, right by his fuse box. He was a respected man in the community and a member of the school board. Again no one spent a night in jail for it. He was just another dead black man in Woodruff County. And as faith would have it, my aunt's husband, Uncle Carlos, came down from California. It had been twenty- six years since they had seen each other. He knew that his health was failing, and he didn't want to die without being with and making things right between him and his wife. So he asked my aunt to move back to California with him, and after raising ten bebes by herself, after the threatening phone call with black folks being killed and nothing being done about it, she was ready to leave Augusta. So after twenty-six long years, my aunt moved back to California. A few years later, her husband died, but my aunt never came back to Woodruff County. It was a legend of how some white men had brutally beaten, raped, cut up, and burned alive a black woman named Ms. Cecily Gates years ago; and that the white guys were seen running from the scene and all of this took place down in the basement of a church. It just so happened the church sat right on the corner of our house that the race-haters burned. So it wasn't anything new about white folks killing blacks. They had heard that before, but never did it happen so fast and so often. Legend has it that the police arrested an innocent black man for it and sent him to prison for it even though people saw the white men running away from the church. That set the tone for blacks not to get involved with whites killing blacks. My best friend Willie and I would still hang out, go to church, and sometimes we would talk to our pastor about what was happening around there between the blacks and the whites. He would tell us to just keep on praying, and he also reminded us of how he first moved there to take a teaching job and that the KKK burned a cross in his yard. And because so many blacks were coming up dead, we knew not to be walking around by ourselves. Willie had started to date a young lady whose name was Isabella Roundtree that lived about ten miles out of town in a little place called Revels. She had just had a baby by him. He, on the other hand, was walking around all proud because he had a little boy, and the girl lived with her parents who lived in a farmhouse. It was said among the blacks that the white owner had asked her dad to move out of that house and off of his land. Willie already knew that they were prejudiced down there. He told me that one night while he was down there visiting his girlfriend and baby that a truckful of white boys came by and start yelling racist slurs, so he told his girlfriend to take the baby and go in the house. He told her that he was going to leave, and as soon as he got in his car and pulled out of the driveway, he noticed some headlights pop on. As he started to drive, they started to follow him and continued yelling racial slurs. The faster he would go, the faster they would go, and this went on all the way back to where he reached the city limits. Now his girlfriend's brother, whose name was Ben Roundtree, was dating a white girl that some say was the mayor of the City of McCrory's daughter, which is still Woodruff County, and that he was being warned to stay away from her. A few days after, they had chased Willie back to town. The brother went out with the white girl again, and somehow he got into it with the Jackson brothers, some white guys that had been telling him to leave her alone. Rumors has it that the white guys followed him home, and once he got home and went inside, they poured gasoline all around the house and set it on fire. They killed Willie's girlfriend, their baby, and his girlfriend's mother; in all eight people of the Roundtree family died that night including Ben. The next morning on the front page of the newspaper, Officer Clefus, the same policeman who hit me and threw me to the ground, was standing in the ashes of the fire and pointing to a crack in the chimney talking about the fire started from a crack in the chimney. He was just a Woodruff County sheriff, not a fire marshal, so that meant that he was definitely not qualified to determine the cause of fire. Again, more blacks had been murdered, and no one was arrested for it; just blacks talking among themselves. Willie was grieving so I tried to say what I could to comfort him. We were terrified of what had happened. We already knew that Officer Clefus Kassie was a dirty cop because it was him who testified at my trial that he hit me and threw me to the ground for no reason and it also was him that told the white girl that if he ever caught us in the woods that he would kill the both of us. Another example of just how dirty Officer Clefus was back to the night of the fire when my family got murdered, my mother had said that she seen the policeman when they picked up something at the front door or at least where the front door used to be and put it in a black garbage bag. And the very next night, after the kids were murdered, they pulled a scare tactic. They sent the police to pick up the people knowing the people were terrified of them because they had proved what they were capable of doing. It would be like you be walking alone, and a limo pulls up and two men getting out and telling you to get in the car in the middle next to Al Capone. I just don't think that it would be a good ride. The fire marshal sent a police car to pick up my mother and my brother Dwayne along with Mrs. Addison Walker and a few others to come up to the Woodruff County Jail so that he could interview them. While my mother was giving a statement, she noticed Officer Clefus standing over by the wall looking in a black garbage bag, closing it, and laughing. After seeing him repeat it over and over, my mother finally asked him what was in the bag and what was so funny. He just simply said that it was confidential, then Mama asked him, "What was so confidential about something that came from my own house and with five kids dead, what could possibility be so funny?" Although she said that to him, he still kept on opening the bag, looking in it, closing it, and laughing. We always thought that it were the cocktails that they threw back at the house as they were running away as Mrs. Addison Walker, who lived right in front of the house, stated in her interview that she had heard something being thrown. While Mrs. Addison Walker was being interviewed, she told the fire marshal that she was awaken by some noises and that she could hear her daughter on the phone with somebody who was insisting to speak to her, but that she kept hearing her daughter saying, "I won't let you speak to her unless you tell me your name." Then she told the fire marshal that she heard the kids screaming and hollering to the top of their lungs for help saying stuff like, "Help, somebody please help us. They're killing us." As she could hear some furniture being thrown and tossed about, she went on to say that she heard three people running and she heard something being thrown back at the house as it made a whistling sound as it was traveling through the air. She heard it hit the front concrete porch with a *ting* sound. She then heard a truck start up with two doors slamming and spinning tires as they pulled off in a hurry and because of the reflection of the fire in her bedroom mirror, she looked out of her window and saw a fire start at the bottom of the front door on the outside of the house as it engulfed the middle of the house. Right where my mother had seen the police pick up whatever it was in that black garbage bags that Officer Clefus Kassie was opening, closing, and laughing at. Now it shouldn't take a rocket scientist to figure out that Mrs. Addison Walker, who was better known as Addie B., actually saw the things that she said that she heard. We later found out that she received a letter warning her not to tell what she saw. The fire marshal would be writing as the people that he was interviewing would be talking, but at the end of each interview, he never asked the people to read and sign what he had wrote to see if they agreed with the statement or not. And that would one day be a problem and after waiting to go to trial for about five years, we received a letter from our lawyer saying that we had finally been scheduled by the court for jury trial in the United States District Court for the Eastern District of Arkansas, and it was set for June 5, 1989 at 9:30 a.m. It was to be held at the United States Post Office and Courts Building at 812 Walnut Street in the city of Helena, Arkansas. It was what we had been waiting for it has been five long agonizing years, and although we were living in Newport, we were still struggling to pay bills, the light bill in particular. So you can imagine what that was was like to lose your family in the dark and still be struggling to stay out of the dark. We knew that suing them was not going to bring the kids back, but it sure would be good not to have to worry about being in the dark again. We were welcoming our days in court and the people were looking to us to change things around there. Ten million dollars were more than most blacks in Woodruff County had ever heard of, less known have. It was definitely our time to shine. Our lawyer pushed to have the trial in Helena instead of Little Rock where it ordinarily supposed to have been held because he thought that since Helena had a lot of blacks living there that we might get more blacks on the jury, and that they might be more sympathetic toward Mama and us as for that mattered. And since the blacks that lived in Augusta were so afraid to testify on our behalf and not wanting anything to do with the trial, he thought that the blacks that didn't live there and wouldn't have to deal with the white folks after the trial might be more understanding, realizing what we had been through and that they might be more willing to rule in our favor. The few blacks who did come from Augusta were only there because they were subpoena and they were saying stuff like "I don't know nothing" and "I don't want to be here" and others were saying, "We still got to live there and I don't want anything to do with this." They were whining so much so until the lawyer told one of them, "Five kids have been murdered and if you know something and don't tell it today, may God have mercy on your soul, so go ahead and leave if you want to," and he left. They were calling us in the courtroom one by one to testify, and Augusta had four lawyers to our one, and anything that our lawyer didn't ask, you could be sure that they did and what little few blacks from Augusta that did stay and took the stand was acting dumbfounded. They were acting like they didn't even know what those white lawyers were talking about. It was most embarrassing what we had for witnesses, but the whites who were there on their behalf were taking the stand and lying, speaking boldly with their testimonies. I couldn't believe what my ears were hearing. They were throwing words around in the courtroom like bombs and explosions, the Ku Klux Klan, and all of them were saying that they were on the scene and had the fire under control, some said in two minutes, and others said in five minutes, but as you look at the pictures, you can only imagine just how much that they were lying in court because it is clear to see that those bodies burned until some of their bones popped out of their skin. Some of them were saying that it was Dale Fallon, who drove the white Ford Pumper fire truck, and that Phil Simpson drove the red Ford cab-over snub-nosed fire truck. And the firefighters were asked what did they do to try to save the kids' life and they replied, "Nothing because the fire was too intense," then our lawyer said to them, "Well if the fire was so hot how did Dwayne go in and out of that house at least three times, but none of you went in once, so what were you all doing?" Then they replied, "We were observing on that part." They was telling the truth because while Eddie and my uncles were trying to cut through the house, the firefighters were just standing around doing nothing. Can you imagine what that night must have been like to know that your family was in there being burned alive and the ones that you hope and trust to help you save their lives, which was what they were trained to do, were not helping you at all. It would be the same as watching someone you love so dear being brutally murdered while the police would be just standing around doing nothing at all to help. And imagine that if someone would have asked them why they didn't do something to help, and they replied that the situation was too dangerous to get involved. The whites were taking the stand and lying about who came to the house and pulled the gas meter, even the manager of the utility company took the stand and lied and said that he was the one who pulled our gas meter, when in fact it was Jeff Row Cox who pulled the meter and stuff like that. Then the chief of police took the stand, and the first thing that he told the court was when he first got the call. They told him that it was a truck on fire on the outskirt of town. I believe that this was done in order to allow the house to burn longer. He testified that they did indeed pull guns on us, and made us stand back and watch the house burn with our family inside. Then the fire marshal took the stand, and as the lawyers that Augusta had hired started to ask him about his credentials, so that they could establish how professional he was, in order to make us look unprofessional or bad in court as if being black and poor wasn't enough, the fire marshal told the court that he had only had one week of bomb training, which meant that he was not qualified to make the call on the explosion, and with a lot of people saying that they heard an explosion including the fireman whose name was Albert Heaney who told the fire marshal that he was awaken out of his sleep by the explosion before the fire call came in. The fire marshal should have notified the Federal Bureau of Investigation, but he didn't. He was also asked by our lawyer what was the cause of fire, and he said that he didn't know, but that he think that it started in the living room by a overstuffed chair, which was another item that the police had thrown out in the yard before the fire marshal arrived. The pathologist made the statement that the kids' blood was cherry red, so our lawyer asked him did he checked them to see if there was cyanide poisoning because that would make the blood cherry red also, and he answer no. People had been saying that they had smelled a foul odor coming from what used to be the front door where the police had picked up something at and put it in that black garbage bag. So our lawyer asked the fire marshal did he check the soil to see if there were any chemicals in it, like gasoline, and the fire marshal lied and said yes. We were there, and we knew that he didn't, because he didn't even have anything to check the soil with, which was the reason that they took the white boy out of jail in the first place, so that they could borrow his tools which was a chainsaw to cut up the floors with, but I can assure you that he didn't have anything that could check some soil with. The truth of the matter was that they were asked by our lawyer not to tear down the house because it was under investigation, but they tore it down in a hurry, and then they took a bulldozer, took up all of the dirt, hauled it off, came back with new dirt, and put it all over where the house used to be. And that was definitely not something that had never happen in Augusta before, nor has it ever happened since. When the Augusta Police took the stand, they were ask why did they pulled guns on us, and they replied that they thought that they heard Eddie say that he was getting a gun, then the lawyer asked, "Where was Eddie going to get it from? It was his house that was on fire." Then they started to ask us about what we had said in a deposition five years ago, and it was then that I realize that they only wanted to know what we knew back then, so that they could use it against us. At the start of the trial, the lawyers were asking the court for a motion to dismiss, but the judge said that it was enough circumstantial evidence to have a trial. But after only two days, they were saying that there was no proof that any Ku Klux Klan member was even in town on the night that my family was murdered. So after just two days, what we had been waiting for, for five long agonizing years was over just like that. Although a few hours earlier, while the jury was still out, they had offered our lawyer one hundred thousand dollars to settle out-of-court before the jury came back and our lawyer turned it down. I mean after all, that was just a drop in the bucket compared to ten million dollars, but the jury came back and didn't give us one dime although one of them was crying to my mother about how sorry he was that they didn't help us out at all. We were leaving Helena with no money and no justice, and even though we had a black judge, it was out of his hands. It was up to the jury, and the jury had spoken. The judge knew that something wasn't right during trial because he had said to Dwayne while he was on the stand, "Tell me what was the real motive for the white folks to kill the kids, and don't say that it's because you're black."

We wanted to tell him that it was because of Eddie Giddy. Eddie had been stealing them white folks farm chemicals and selling them to other white farmers, and Warnell had stolen a garbage of weed from the jail, so in reality, they were retaliating but we didn't want to send Warnell and Eddie to jail, knowing that if we would expose them in court and go back to Augusta with them knowing for sure that they had did it, they would not have stopped until they had killed them for sure. It was too much to risk. So we went back home with no hope for justice. We used to have a court date to look forward to, but now even that was gone. And the blacks in Woodruff County who had high hopes that things were going to change knew that things were going to remain the same. We looked like just another black family that was no different from any other black families who were murdered in Woodruff County. The white folks could kill our family and get away with it too. Now, we were afraid that they were going to retaliate on us for even trying to file a lawsuit against them. It was front-page news in the Augusta Advocate the very next morning after the trial in big bold letters: Augusta Won Lawsuit Over Paula Armstrong. Many of the blacks in that town looked up to my mother because when food stamps first came out, the white folks didn't tell the blacks anything about them. They didn't even let them know that they could apply for them or that they were available. It just so happened that Mama wrote a letter to the governor who, I believe was Forbs at that time, telling him that her husband was locked up in prison and that she needed some help taking care of her small children, so he wrote her back and simply told her to go to the local social service and apply for food stamps, and so she did. So can you imagine what the other black folks were thinking in a time when they had to pay cash for everything and could not afford to have meat at every meal found out that my mother had walked up in social service and got some kind of new currency that she could go to the store with and buy any kinds of food that she wanted. Eventually, the word got around, and in a little while it seem like every black person in Augusta was spending some food stamps. So you can see how and why the blacks would look up to her, plus she had gone from the projects to owning her own brick home. But after the trial, once again we were embarrassed. We had openly challenged them white folks, and we had failed. But I was always taught those if you try once and don't succeed, try and try again. I knew in my heart that if I would have been murdered, Otis would not have stopped trying to get justice for me, and the thought of that alone has compelled me to search high and low over 30 years for justice. A lot of things happened down there in Helena in court that have stayed with me until this day, like when Mrs. Addison Walker testified under oath in the United States District Court that she had told the fire marshal that when he interviewed her that she heard three people running and something being thrown back at the house, and how she saw the fire start at the bottom of the front door on the outside of the house, and the same fireman Mr. Phil Simpson, who drove the red Ford fire truck, said that he saw the fire burning at the bottom of the front door on the outside when he first got on the scene, but that the fire marshal had intentionally left all of that out of his report. Another thing that has stayed with me through the years was the thing that the white boy whom they got out of jail, Richard James, said and that was that the Ku Klux Klan had killed the kids and that he was in the police car with Captain Linden Dirk of the Augusta Police Department when the call from the state medical examiner office came over the police scanner. Dr. Milton Holliday said that we are going to say that all of them died of smoke inhalation. And when we told that to the court, the lawyers who were working for Augusta laughed at us saying that we should not make those kinds of allegations on the state pathologist, but we had been told by Richard James that the state pathologist was paid fifteen thousand dollars to falsify the autopsy reports. This was in 1989 when we told it to the courts, but we had known it ever since a few days after the kids got killed, when Richard James first told us about Dr. Milton Holliday. But on Saturday, November 7, 1992, the *Arkansas Democrat-Gazette* reported that two independent pathologists were hired to review fourteen autopsies that was conducted at the Arkansas State Crime Laboratory by Dr. Milton Holliday. They had concluded that incorrect results were reached in four cases. The pathologists agreed that the cause of the 1989 death of Betty Jean Snips of Searcy County should be labeled as "undetermined" because Milton Holliday had determined that Betty Jean Snips died from injuries that incurred by falling from a thirteen-inch- high porch, but Snips parents' contended that she was beaten to death. In the following cases, the pathologists agreed that the manner of death was undetermined in the 1987 shooting, death of Chris Gamble of Little Rock. Milton Holliday had originally ruled the death a suicide, but later after examining new information, he said that the cause was not to be determined. But the independent pathologists said that the manner of death was a homicide, and again there was the 1985 death of David Hasselbeck of Mountain Home, who was shot once in the head and four times in the chest, and Milton Holliday ruled that the death was a suicide, but the pathologists said that the manner of death could not be determined. I mean, come on, what are the chances of someone falling off a porch that is barely over one foot tall and killing themselves to the point that they look like they were beaten to death, or tell me who can commit a suicide by shooting himself once in the head and then shoot himself four more times in the chest or vice versa. Also in 1987, Ralph and Craig Houston were hit by a train, and Milton Holliday concluded that the boys were hit after they had smoked some marijuana and fell asleep on the railroad tracks, but the other pathologists concluded that they were hit in the head with the butt of a shotgun and a grand jury later ruled that their deaths were homicide. I can only wonder what do those lawyers, who laughed at us that day in court, when we told them that the state pathologist was making fake reports think of us now. In September 1991, Dr. Milton Holliday was forced by Alvin Berry who at that time was Govenor to resign amid controversial complaints that he had botched up autopsy results. Dr. Milton made the newspapers again by seeking an examiner job in Guam which is a United States trust territory island in the Southern Marianas. The papers said that Holliday's chances of landing the new job may have paled because of apparent inconsistencies in his resume. In other words, he was caught lying on his resume. Now you can clearly see why we believe that he botched up our family autopsy reports as well especially since we were the first to say that he was making up false autopsies and giving inaccurate testimonies. On March 19, 1992, which was about three years after we had lost in court, our attorney wrote a letter to the Honorable Ned Hunt who at that time was the prosecuting attorney, and asked him if he would support him in getting an investigation because the autopsy was performed by Dr. Holliday and that he did not conduct test to see if the children had been killed prior to the fire, nor did he conduct any tests to see had the children been burned as a result of flammable liquids or any other substance. The attorney also said in that same letter that he had received numerous telephone calls from anonymous white residences of Augusta, Woodruff County, who assured that this was in fact a murder, and that if an investigation was conducted and if they got those bodies up then the evidence would come forward. Our attorney had requested a criminal investigation of the arson and murder from the prosecuting attorney's office and from the law enforcement officials in Augusta, but the state fire marshal ruled the fire an accident so if it was said to be an accident then those officials would not have to look for a murderer. So the Augusta police went with the ruling of an accident and refused to investigate any further. So we never got that investigation, and it was back to business as usual in Woodruff County. But all was not doom and gloom. I married Velma Jean Houston, the girl that I had met in Newport, and that has been twenty-nine years ago, and in about a year and a half later, my best friend Willie met my wife's sister and married her. In about a couple of years later, my cousin Boomer met our wife's niece and married her just like we had said one night while we were walking up and down the street in front of our houses fantasizing in Woodruff County. And because we had hit a dead-end street with the case about the kids, I was ready to leave Arkansas. I had had enough so in November 1992 on the same night that former President Alvin Berry was declared president-elect, I left Arkansas and moved to Rochester, New York, which was another part of our fantasy that came true. I can imagine what those slaves felt after they had left the dirty south and made it to freedom, because when I first made it to New York, I somewhat felt as if I had just escaped slavery and made it to freedom. It was so different from the dirty south, the blacks and whites had been getting along there for years, some were even married. Don't get me wrong, you can always find someone that's nasty, but for the most part, the relationships were good, and Rochester was a city that was rich with American history. Eventually, I landed a good job with a Fortune 500 company named Xerox, and bought my first house on the west side of the city at 267 Post Avenue. It was just a hop, skip, and a jump from the Susan B. Anthony house. Right down the street from my house, on my street, I noticed a sign one day that read: This House was a Part of the Underground Railroad.

Can you even imagine how proud I was to know that I had brought a house on a street that Harriet Tubman might have been on. And only a few minutes from the church that the late great Frederick Douglass would publish his *North Star* newspaper from down town Rochester. It was like a dream come true. I had achieved the American dream. And even though I was now living in a city that was rich with American history, every now and then, I would receive word from down south that another black had been found dead at the hand of some white man. No investigation and no one spend a night in jail as long as the victims are black. But let'S look at this case, one night at a football game, a black guy got into a fight with a white guy and another white guy tried to hit the black guy with a baseball bat, but he stuck the white guy in the head instead and because some other black guys saw that, it was more than one white fight, they got in it too. But when it was all over, they took the white guy that the other white guy had hit in the head to the hospital, but he later died; and guess what, they charged all five blacks guys with murder even though it was only one bat and another white guy had that; the black guys were the ones that got the charged and went to the Woodruff County Jail. It wasn't until later that the charges were dropped when the truth finally came out. I hate that, that young man lost his life, and I am not saying that if it was a black guy that he should not have been held accountable because he should, but so should the whites when a black comes up dead. Like when I got the call from down south that Emma Lakes had been picked up and arrested. This Emma Lakes was the same girl that I had asked to drive my car that night when the white boy was talking about shooting me point blank while I was trying not to faint. They told me that she was yelling and kicking the bars in the Woodruff County Jail when Billy Earl made the statement that he would shut her up and then he went back to Emma's jail cell. The next thing everybody knew Emma Lakes was found dead hanging in her jail cell. I went to a Arkansas reunion in Memphis back in August 2013, and I saw one of the former black cops there. They were telling me that the thing that Emma hung herself with was too small to do use for that, and that they still had a picture of it. Also the coroner donated a vault to preserve her body just in case it is ever investigated. I went to jail on October 31, 1987, and who would have ever thought that all of those years later, the same white guy that had tried to kill me and got me sent to jail would actually kill Emma in jail. Although I had moved to New York, still a part of me longed for my people, and my native land, and it was my desire that my people would come to experience the freedom that New York had to offer, which I had come to know and love. Although we had lost in court with a verdict for the defendant, I still had a yearning for justice deep down in my soul; something like what Harriet had for freedom. She not only wanted it for herself, but risking her own freedom and life so that someone else might experience it as well. One day while I was at work at Xerox, I picked up a newspaper and saw an article on a Mr. Nicolas King of a new Monroe County Chapter Southern Christian Leadership Conference also known as the SCLC, which was started back in 1958 by Dr. Frederick Lee Miller Jr. I was already familiar with the SCLC because after that we had lost in court, I worked and saved up enough money to pay for gas and hotel to take my mother and two carloads of us to go to the SCLC headquarters in Atlanta, Georgia, and had a sit-down with a gentlemen by the name of Mr. A. C. Cotton Reader. I never forgot that name. I was trying to find justice anyway that I could. I even drove down to Montgomery, Alabama, to the Southern Poverty Law Center to see if I could meet and at least talk with a Mr. Dwight Douglas. but being inexperience and not knowing what time to leave so that you could arrive at a certain time, I got there around midnight and the center was closed, so I just left the documents to the security guard to give them to Mr. Dwight Douglas for me. I could not afford to stay. I only had enough money to buy gas and food to get us back home in Arkansas, which by the way, I never heard from Mr. Douglas. So when I saw the article in the newspaper that said that the SCLC had establish a chapter right here in Rochester, I could hardly wait to get out of work to call and go and talk with him. When I called,

Mr. Nicolas King answered so I told him who I was and then I began to tell him all about what had happen to my family back in Woodruff County, Arkansas. So he set me up with an appointment to meet with him, and to show him what documents I had to support my story, like newspaper clippings, court documents, and so forth. However, I was so glad that I had found someone who was actually interested in the case and was willing to help me until I went to Arkansas to tell my mother and family the good news and all. But because I was down there, I missed my appointment with him. As soon as I got back to Rochester, I called and made another appointment with him. We agreed to meet on the east side of the city what was at that time the newly built McDonald's that was located on Upper Falls Boulevard, because it was the one place in the city of Rochester that we both knew how to get to. I was sitting in there anxiously waiting to meet him then these two men came in. One of them I had seen before on television talking about the Rochester school board, but the other one looked like the picture that I had seen in the newspaper. He was kind of heavyset, big-eyed with a mixture of black and gray hair, and I said to myself this must be him and it was. We introduced ourselves, and I began to tell him the story. He looked at the papers that I had, and asked me if I had any more. Then he began to talk to me real rough then he would ask me about this and about that over and over again until I just thought that he didn't believe me, and all of a sudden, I began to feel that this was just another time that I had gotten my hopes up high for nothing.

Then I started to cry as we yelled back and forth at each other. I was trying to convince him that I was telling him the truth about how my family had been murdered and that I was not just a family member out for revenge, but that no one was actually been held responsible for the murdering of my family. But he was yelling at me telling me not to be wasting his time. And even I will admit and be the first to say that being told and hearing for the very first time that a state medical examiner, a state fire marshal, a town coroner, the city of Augusta, the city of Patterson, and the Woodruff County Police and the Augusta Fire Department all played their part in one of the greatest racial murder cover-ups with "cover-up" being the key word in the history of America is a hard, very hard, bitter pill to swallow. It was a complicated case, because the authorities were the accused. If someone throws a rock and breaks your window, you can call the police, but who do you call if it's the police throwing the rocks. Mr. Nicolas King started to walk out on me then he turned to me and said that I needed more documents. I knew that I needed his help and that for me to get the documents that he wanted meant that I would have to go back to Arkansas to get the information that he needed. So even with the SCLC being right in Rochester, New York, I would still have to make long trips to try and make this work. But as he was walking out, I said to him, "That's all right if you don't want to help me, I'm not going to give up, God will help me get an investigation with or without you." I didn't find out until later after that we had become good friends, and that when I had said that to him that was the moment that convinced him to believe me and that I was telling him the truth. I went back to Arkansas again and came back with the information that Mr. Nicolas King wanted and needed. So he started to make some phone calls and when he called the main office of the SCLC in Atlanta, I knew then that he was not playing around and that he was really on the case. He told them about the case, that he was acting on it, and they gave him permission to act. I had already went to a member of congress and she in return sent a letter to the Honorable Kate Songs, who was at that time the attorney general of the United States Department of Justice, and she told her in a letter that I myself believed that the Ku Klux Klan had in fact murdered my family. And those Klan activities were still continuing in Woodruff County, Arkansas. And that I believed that the local officials in the city of Augusta, Arkansas, had participated in a cover-up of the incident. This was January 27, 1997, and on September 3, 1997, I received a letter stating that they regret that the response could not have been more favorable and the letter came from the United States Department of Justice Civil Rights Division. It was most definitely not the news that we were expecting or wanted to hear. I knew that I just couldn't stop trying to bring about an investigation, and so I didn't. I wrote a letter to *Ebony* magazine hoping to, at the least, get the story out. But on January 21, 1998, I got a letter back from *Ebony* thanking me for my interest and that my suggestion would be discussed at the next meeting of the *Ebony* editorial board and that they would be in touch with me if they were going to schedule the story, but if I didn't hear from them in four weeks then that would mean that they could not schedule the story at that time. Tragically, I never heard from them. On January 29, 1998, I received a personal letter from Congresswoman Dolly Lawson telling me that she had contacted the Honorable Kate Songs on behalf of my family and me. She said that she could certainly understand my concern with this matter. So I went back to Arkansas just to tell everyone that I was still trying to have something done about it. And while I was in Arkansas, Woodruff County, they told me that another black man had been killed over a white girl by the Woodruff County police along with the Arkansas State Police and the Jackson County Police, but this time, they castrated him. So on Thursday, February 5, 1998, the *Arkansas Democrat-Gazette* headline these words on page six: B-Police Maliciously Slew Man at Roadblock Suit Claims. The newspaper reported that the lawsuit alleges that the officers violated several federal laws being the first, fourth, fifth, eighth, and fourteenth amendments of the United States Constitution the report went on to say that the defendants took aim with their weapons and without legal justification, willfully, maliciously, and intentionally fired their weapons at Dean, hitting him on the left side of the head, the lawsuit says. The lawsuit contends that Mr. Dean was taken away by an ambulance to an unknown place where he was castrated and some body parts where removed without the family's permission. It was business as usual in Woodruff County. Blacks were still being murdered by whites and wasn't a thing being done about it. Rumors has it that they took his body to the town of Newport to a black-owned funeral home, and it is said that when they threw his body on the table that the funeral director, when he saw the horrible condition that it was in, he ran out of the backdoor of the funeral home and called the Federal Bureau of Investigation. Also while I was in Arkansas, I met with the Jackson County branch president of the National Association for the Advancement of Colored People (NAACP). He told me about the wrongful death of Mr. Dean and that he would be willing to give me a letter of support about the murdering of my family in hopes that it would help us get the investigation. So on December 4, 1999, the branch president of the NAACP prepared a letter to the SCLC on my behalf and it was also during that time when he gave me the connection to a law professor that lived in Hamden, Connecticut, who was teaching law at what was then Quinnipiac College School of Law, before it became Quinnipiac University. I was putting together a team a civil rights worker, who had marched with Dr. Frederick Lee Miller Jr. himself and a law professor that knew the law so well that she was teaching students to be lawyers. When I got back from Arkansas, I gave the information to Mr. Nicolas King about the law professor that the branch president had recommended me to contact. Mr. Nicolas King called Professor Elizabeth Franklin, and they began to communicate. Mr. King also wrote to another member of congress, House of Representatives Mr. Dan Robertson. We were reaching out to anybody that we thought would be willing to help us out. Mr. Nicolas King thought that because Mr. Robertson had spoken out against former president Alvin Berry and because the tragedy had happened back in Arkansas on his watch, that Mr. Dan Robertson might take that as an opportunity to make the case world-renowned. And on my thirty-ninth birthday, October 22, 1999, I received a response from Congressman Robertson who said that his heart truly went out to my family and me, and that after reading the material that we had provided him, he called the Arkansas Department of Health to inquire about the process that an individual would need to go through to request that a body be exhumed. And that we should contact that office and request a form for disinterment, and so we did. He also informed us that he had contacted Congressman Benjamin Lane who was the United States representative for the first congressional district of Arkansas which I believe also covers Woodruff County along with a letter indicating his willingness to help in any way he could. Mr. King felt that he needed to create a paper trail, so we contacted the attorney that had handled the case and on December 16, 1999, Mr. Samuel Wright responded to Mr. Nicolas King in a letter that said that he had handled the case for my mother and that it was a federal case that was held in District Court for the Eastern District of Arkansas. He said that the jury had returned a verdict for the defendants, but that he believes then as he still believes now that the children died as a result of a homicide. He went on to say in the letter that the medical examiner due to the fire marshal's report ruled the deaths accidental. But that it was in his opinion that the bodies must be exhumed and examined by a competent professional to determine the cause of death before an investigation can proceed. And being reminded of the closing statements that the plaintiffs' lawyers made at the end of trial to the court in 1989 saying that there was no proof that any Ku Klux Klan was even in Augusta when my family was murdered and that there was no proof that any Klan activities were going on in the area. But around 2001, the Ku Klux Klan marched the streets of Augusta all the way up to the Woodruff County courthouse. They were talking over the loudspeakers calling black peoples the "n" word as they were trying to recruit new Klan members. It was the talk of the town. They had come out of hiding. It was no longer a reason to wonder or guess if the Klan were still in the area. And while all of that was taking place in the south, Mr. Nicolas King back east was still building a paper trail. On Tuesday, January 4, 2000, Mr. King himself wrote a letter to Attorney General Kate Songs and told her that he had been working with her agencies from different parts of the country. After that, he had identified himself. He then told her that based upon our investigation we had concluded that there was foul play, and that the government officials locally and statewide acted in concert and individually to cover up the murder of five innocent children. He then asked her to launch a vigorous investigation to find out what really happened in Augusta, Woodruff County, on the night of March 2, 1984. He told her that he was awaiting her unselfish response and then he ended his letter with these words: Love Embraces Justice. One day, Mr. King asked me to go with him because he wanted me to meet someone that he said was a very good friend of his. It turned out to be none other than the late great Reverend Jacob Cobs. I learned that Reverend Cobs had been fighting racism almost single-handed before Mr. King came to Rochester, but now he served as the chairman of the Monroe County Chapter of the SCLE. Reverend Jacob Cobs had been active in civil rights in and around Rochester for a very long time. He also was one of the original protesters that chained up the doors of the Colgate Rochester Crozer Divinity

School. They had locked the school down by putting locks and chains on the doors, not letting anyone in or out of the school. They stayed in the school like that for a week or more; and let me remind you that they were teaching the Bible at that school, but they were still racists. As Reverend Cobs was telling me his story, I found it to be amazing how that they could teach the Word of God and be so educated in the Word, but yet cannot understand that God made all men equal. Then Mr. Nicolas King wanted me to tell Reverend Jacob Cobs my story, so I did. After I had finished telling him what had happen to my family, he said that he would write a letter to the department of justice also asking for an investigation. So on January 8, 2000, Reverend Cobs wrote a letter to Attorney General Kate Songs. He told her in the letter that he was soliciting her support and influence in securing justice about the murder and cover-up which was the order of the day. He proceeded to introduce himself as the president of the United Church Ministry Incorporation, which was an organization comprised of approximately eighty churches. He went on to say that as a Christian organization, justice has not been served on the perpetrators of those horrible deaths and crimes. Then he too asked her to launch a vigorous investigation to determine just what had happened in Augusta, Woodruff County, in the cover of night on March 2, 1984. So as you can see it was a team effort to bring about justice. And on January 11, 2000, I went to Syracuse, New York, and I hired a forensic consulting expert by the name of Langston Grayson at forty-five dollars an hour, and I gave him a copy of all of the documents that I had at the time I had kept down through the years. And after I had given her a couple of months with them, I called him up to see what he thought, and he wanted me to come and see him. At first, he was telling me that according to the documents, he believes that it was foul play. But then I told him that the news reporters was going to put his finding on television, and that this was going to hit the news. Then he changed his tone and said, "Well if they did all what they were supposed to do then they did the right thing, but if they didn't do all what they were supposed to do then they did the wrong thing." So he simply just straddled the fence on me and all of that money that I had paid him. I got nothing for it. At least nothing that I could use to get the investigation with. But I still couldn't give up. One day, I saw in the newspapers that the man that I had drove all the way to Montgomery, Alabama, to see some years ago was coming to Rochester on Monday, January 17, 2000, and by then my family had been dead for about sixteen years. Now Mr. Dwight Douglas was going to be the guest speaker at the art center that was called the Callahan Theater at Nazareth College to celebrate Dr. Frederick Lee Miller Jr. Day, so I told Mr. Nicolas King that we needed to go to Nazareth College to meet and talk to Mr. Douglas, but Mr. King was sick and didn't feel like going, so I told him that I would go and see if I could get a chance to talk with Mr. Douglas. I knew that we needed him on our team because he was one of the biggest and greatest civil rights attorneys on the planet. I knew if anybody could help us, he could. Because in my studying, I learn that Dwight Douglas was born in 1936 in Shorter, Alabama. He was the son of a farmer and a cotton gin operator. He was a very active young man in high school and was named the star farmer of Alabama in 1955 by the Alabama Future Farmers of America. Dwight Douglas had attended an undergraduate school at the University of Alabama, where he founded a nationwide mail sales company that specialized in book publishing after he graduated from the University of Alabama School of Law in 1960. He returned to Montgomery, Alabama, where he opened a law office and still continued his mail-order business. The direct mail publishing business was a hit. Lucas and Douglas Marketing Group turned out to be one of the largest publishing companies in the south. The company pioneered mail sales of long overdue children sex education books. It's the new horizon division published the National Aeronautics and Space Administration (NASA) and the Smithsonian Institution. Sales went as high as fifteen million and by 1969, Dwight Douglas sold the company to *Times*. In recognition of his published work and his hard efforts to encourage young people to become more active in the business world, he was named one of the ten outstanding young men of America in 1966 by the United States Jaycees. It was during the civil rights moment when Mr. Douglas first became active aiding minorities in the courtrooms. In 1967, he filed suit to stop construction of a white university in a city in Alabama that had a predominantly black state college. Like I said, if he could not help me then I didn't know who could. Also in 1968, Mr. Douglas filed a suit to integrate the all-white YMCA in the city of Montgomery along with Harry Goodman and Javier Lumpkin. Mr. Douglas also had founded the Southern Poverty Law Center in Montgomery in 1971. This center supported by contributions from almost five hundred thousand citizens across the nation and has engaged in civil rights lawsuits ranging from the defense of Joan Little in North Carolina to the integration of the Alabama State Troopers. Another reason that we needed him on our team was because in 1980, the Southern Poverty Law Center founded Klanwatch in response to a resurgence racist activity. The project monitors hate groups and develops legal strategies for protecting citizens from violence-prone groups. And on January 25, 1991, a television film about Mr. Douglas aired on *NBC*. "Line of Fire" describes his successful fight against the Ku Klux Klan, which also include the seven-million dollar precedent setting judgment against the United Klans of America on behalf of the mother of Stefan Hollis, a young black man that the Ku Klux Klan lynched in Mobile, Alabama. In order for him to help educate young people about the civil rights movement, he developed the idea for the Civil Rights Memorial which was designed by Delia Harrison. The memorial bears the names of the forty men, women, and children, who lost their lives during the civil rights movement. At least ten thousand people attended the dedication of the memorial in Montgomery in 1989. This man has received numerous honors and awards in conjunction with his work at the center. Mr. Douglas was named the trial lawyer of the year by trial lawyers for public justice in 1987. He received the Public Service Achievement Award from Common Cause in 1988 and the Roger Baldwin Award from the American Civil Liberties Union in 1989. He was also given the Martin Luther King Jr. Memorial Award by the National Education Association in 1990. It really would look like Mr. Dwight Douglas had received every reward that the civil rights movement had to offer, but it didn't stop there, he was also given the Barbara Jordan Award from the Hollywood Women's Political Committee in 1991, the William O. Douglas Prize from public counsel in 1992, the First Amendment Award from the Houston Trial Lawyers Foundation in 1996, the Civil Rights Award from the National Bar Association in

1998, and the Faith and Humanity Award from the National Council of Jewish Women in 1999. It was in May 1991 when Mr. Douglas received a Special Humanitarian Award from the Direct Marketing Day in New York in recognition of the skillful application of his own direct marketing talents for the principles of justice and fair play through his work at the Southern Poverty Law Center. As if that wasn't enough, in 1998, he was named to the Direct Marketing Association Hall of Fame. In addition to applying his direct mail marketing skills to raising money for civil rights activities, he revolutionized political fundraising in 1992. As the finance director, he raised over twenty-four million dollars from six hundred thousand small donors. This was the first time ever that a presidential campaign had been financed with small gifts by mail. In 1976, Mr. Douglas served as then-president Harvey's national finance director and as a national finance chairman for Senator Cristiano's 1980 presidential campaigns. He also was the chief trial counsel and chair of the committee for the Southern Poverty Law Center. He had devoted his life and time to suing violent white supremacist groups and developing ideas for teaching tolerance, the centers education project. The center has distributed free to schools over three million *Teaching Tolerance* magazines and more than fifty-five teaching kits of each of the first and second in a series of six video and text tolerance education kit. The video in the first kit—*A Time for Justice* won an academy award for Documentary Short Subject in 1995. The video in the second kid— *The Shadow of Hate: A History of Intolerance in America* was nominated for Best Documentary Short in 1996. His autobiography, *A Season For Justice*, was published by Longabaugh and Friedman in 1991 hate on trial, and the case against America's most dangerous neo-Nazi was published by Early Morning Learning in 1993, *Hate on Trial Chronicles*. The trial and twelve-and-a-half million judgments against white supremacist Archie Armengol and his white Aryan resistance group for their responsibility in the beating to death by skinheads of a young black student in Portland, Oregon. The book, *Gathering Storm: America's Militia Threat*, exposes the danger posed by today's domestic terrorist groups. It was published by Brett and Brett publishers. In the movie, *Line of Fire*, actor Corbin Bern son portrayed Mr. Douglas in the film. *Ghosts of Mississippi*, a film that was released back in 1996, was about the life of slain civil rights worker Howell Black. He was portrayed by actor Petros Day, and again, I say if anybody could have helped us with this case, surely he could have. Hope was rising. I had been waiting even though I could hardly wait until the seventeenth. But it had come and I had told Mr. King that I was going, so I went. I was in the building, but I was kind of far back. But I could see him, and I was listening to him as he was speaking. The place was full of people and I was ready, this was it. This was my chance to get the help that my family and I so desperately needed. Slowly the night wind down and finally it came to a close. People were clapping and rushing down to talk to him and shake his hand. I got in the crowd as they form a long line and one by one people were getting their chance to meet him. Finally, it was my moment. I shook his hand as I introduced myself then I began to tell him about the murdering of my family. I was trying to tell him as much important stuff as fast as I could while I had his attention. Others were waiting, but they could tell that he was very interested in what I was telling him. He was asking me about this and that, and for a moment, I thought that I had done it. I had gotten one of the best in the business to join our team. It started to look like he was going to help me, but then it happened. I told him that we had gone to trial already on June 5, 1989, and that this matter had gone to trial before a jury in which a verdict was rendered for the defendant, then he gave me this look. He then picked up a copy of the program, signed it, and gave it to me. It was a signed autograph that read: To Kent Handy Good Luck, Dwight Douglas. My uncle back in Arkansas was the first one to tell me about him, and I thought for sure that I was going to go back home and tell Mr. Nicolas King and my family the good news that he was going to help us, but instead I went back home knowing that he was not going to help us. Because we had already gone to trial and lost, and that meant that he would have to take it all the way to the supreme court, and although he had a very impressive civil rights record, I had never seen where he ever took a case all the way to the supreme court, so my only guess was that was more than he was even willing to do. So why do I even keep looking for justice? I'll tell you why, because it's the right thing to do even against all odds.

And I will be the first to tell you that it's not always easy to get justice when you are limited with an education, it is not always easy to find justice when you are poor, and Lord knows that it's not always easy to find justice when you are black. And I have learned that she doesn't always come swift. On March 2, 2014, it will be thirty years. I have been looking for her for a long time now, but I know that she will never change. I believe that one day she will show her face, and on that day, I will recognize her as justice. I was the spokesperson for my family, and for whatever reason, all of my family looked to me to get something done about it. Otis was my aunt's only son, and whenever I would go to the dirty south, she seem to never fail to ask me what was I doing about it—meaning his death—and holidays were the worse and it didn't matter which holiday because the kids were so young when they were murdered even Halloween was a reminder of who we had lost. I, meanwhile, had a family of my own, so it wasn't easy to be a husband, a dad, and just trying to have a life of my own and at the same time trying to find justice for my family as a whole. By me living in New York, sometimes I would get lonely and want to go to Woodruff County to see my family, but because I didn't have no new news, I would just stay in New York. Over the years, occasionally I would go home and spend Christmas with my mother. After she would prepare her Christmas dinner, she would say, "I wish that my babies were here to enjoy this meal with us, because when they died I was not able to cook. I had no lights, no water, no gas." So what used to be a time for us to come together and show our love became a time to grieve. Living with knowing that my family was murdered and with almost everything being a constant reminder was another reason that I had to look for justice. I have to look for her until she shows her face, or until I take my last breathe, whichever comes first. Ten days after I met with Mr. Douglas, on January 27, 2000, my lawyer, the law professor, Elizabeth Franklin, sent a letter to the fire department chief of Augusta, Woodruff County, asking him to forward any and all documents regarding the investigation, examinations, and reports to her. And on that same day, she requested all documents from the Augusta, Woodruff County, Police Department and to the chief of police. And because I lived in New York and my mom and aunt lived in the dirty south, it made it hard to get the papers signed that the lawyers needed. We would have to mail them down to Arkansas and have them sign them and then mail them back to us. And that was taking too much time, so on February 1, 2000, my mom and my aunt gave me power of attorney, so that I could just handle everything from New York. And although we didn't get Mr. Douglas on our team, we were still making progress. We had already gone through the process regarding the letter of Congressman Dan Robertson and contacted the Arkansas State Department of Health officials and requested the forms for disinterment. About two hours after that, Mr. Nicolas King and I faxed over the request. It was evaluated at the state level, and on December 13, 1999, the state of Arkansas approved our request. That was one victory of the many battles that we would encounter. It was an uphill battle, because in order to get those bodies up, we would need some money to get new caskets to rebury them and a funeral home that would take them once we got them up. And most of all, we needed a competent pathologist to do the examining, and we needed one that did not live or work in Arkansas. so Mr. King began to search the county for a pathologist with most of whom we found were either too involved in other cases or the case was too faraway for them to close their offices and go to where the bodies were. Plus Mr. King was asking them to do it for little or no money at all. But sometimes what you are looking for can be right in front of your face. Mr. Nicolas King placed a call to Strong Memorial Hospital and spoke to the head medical examiner, Dr. Langston Grayson, who in return referred him to a pathologist who was so good that he himself used him from time to time and that pathologist office was less than a hundred miles away. Mr. King contacted him, and he agreed to do the exemptions. And for us, that was another victory and a weight off our shoulder. We were making progress. Dr. Grayson requested all documents and records, but Mr. Nicolas King or myself could not obtain them, so we had to call the law professor, and she made the request for us. Things were starting to look good about the case, and I stayed in contact with my family down south letting them know that we were finally making some real progress. Although Mr. King had never met my mother, he would often talk to her by phone. He was telling them that all he was looking forward to meeting them when we came to Arkansas to get the bodies up. He was also telling them that he was looking forward to eating some of their good old down-south cooking. But like anything else, there is no victory without conflict, and it is often said that if there is no pain, there is no gain. Mr. King lived in an upstairs apartment on the east side of the city. One day, he and the people who lived downstairs had a disagreement about the driveway and even though he lived there first, the landlord made a deal with the people downstairs to sell them the whole house. So they asked Mr. Nicolas King to move out right away, and with him being on the go all the time for other people with such short notice, he had to put his things in storage and stay in a hotel. So I thought to myself that this man has done more for me and my family on this case than anybody. I can't have him living out of any hotel so I asked him to come and live with me and my family. He accepted my offer. I told him that God wanted us to be together, and from that time on, Mr. King was like a father to me. And in many ways, he reminded me of my father. I can still remember waking up early in the morning to go to work, and when I would come out of my bedroom into the hallway, I would see a light at the bottom of his bedroom door. I would ask him, "Are you up, Doc?" and he would answer, "Yeah I'm up," then we would exchange good mornings. After which, he would begin to tell me all about his plans for that day. You know like who he was going to contact and so forth. In the evening when I would return from work, he would tell me all about his accomplishments and we both would be excited. Almost every Saturday, we would look forward to going out to breakfast, but some mornings, my wife would stay in bed, and it would just be he and I who would go out to eat. We would be talking and laughing about everything, and some of it was in the past. Sometimes he would be telling me about things that happened even before I was born. I could tell him anything, and I still cherished those moments. I was sitting down with a civil rights giant, one that had marched with Dr. Frederick Lee Miller Jr. himself. Mr. King was from Florida, and he was familiar with the hate crimes in that area. He was the chapter president of the SCLC at Fort Walton Beach for twelve years. So he knew the history of some of the hate crimes, like the movie *Rosewood* that was based on a true story. How a town in Florida was booming where blacks owned their own homes and businesses during a time in American history when many blacks down south was no more than a sharecropper. However, all of that would change when just one white woman reported that she had been raped by a black man to an angry mob of white men who have taken the law into their own hands and hanged, shot, and lynched many of the black men, women, and children. And then they burned the whole town down to the ground. Mr. Nicolas King and I would talk about stuff like the Greenwood District of Tulsa, Oklahoma, from the early 1900s until 1921 was known as the Black Wall Street. It was also said to have been the richest predominantly black communities in the United States. That was until May 30, 1921, when again just one white woman said that a black allegedly assaulted her. And when the word got out, he was arrested and jailed. About two thousand angry whites gathered outside the courthouse. Rumors of a possible hanging promoted about a hundred black men to come to the jail to protect him and a confrontation took place, gunshots rang out, a riot had started, and it went from downtown to the Greenwood District area where whites broke into stores, stealing, and destroying properties. About ten thousand whites had descended upon Greenwood while homes and businesses went up into flames. Authorities rounded up many of the blacks and took them to internment cemeteries. And by the time that martial law was established, homes, churches, and businesses had been looted and burned to the ground. Even though there is no accurate death count, the number ranged anywhere from twenty-seven to three hundred, according to the report. It is said that the race riot in Tulsa was one of the deadliest in American history. And although those things happened before I was born, I still had a few stories of my own to share with Mr. King. Like the one that a friend of mine from Mississippi told me about how his mother got hit by a car and was lying on the side of the road, and when the ambulance came and saw that she was black, they would not pick her up and said that she would have to wait for the ambulance for colored people to come and get her. They would not help her so she died on the side of that road that day all because she was black. They would not let her ride in that whites-only ambulance. Mr. King was impressed with me because I had survived my family's tragedy, and I was impressed with him and his life. He and I had gotten real close we could talk and tell each other anything. I was always meeting new people because he was the branch president of the SCLC Monroe Chapter and because he lived with me, some very famous people would call my home, such as Frederick Lee Miller III, who at that time was the national president of the Southern Christian Leadership Conference (SCLC), and Mr. Jeffry Alardo who worked for the Center for Constitutional Rights, then there was Mr. Mike Dancer, NAACP Legal Defense Fund, and last but not least, the activist Wyatt Fisher, and Reverend Anthony Goldwater, who was the president of National Action Network was calling my home as well. Mr. Nicolas King had told me that he was born on June 15, 1940, in a small town called Bradenton, Florida, but he grew up in Palmetto, Florida, where he attended Lincoln Memorial High School. And that as a teenager in Florida, he was troubled by the racism that he had experienced and was inspired by Dr. Frederick Lee Miller Jr. This motivation made him become involved in the civil rights movement that swept the nation, which led him to be present at the March on Washington that was led by Dr. Frederick Lee Miller Jr. in 1957. Mr. Nicolas King told me that he had begun his journey traveling to and from Western New York as he was becoming a migrant worker picking fruit in Sodus, Wayne County. And as he would visit the city of Rochester on the weekends he also landed a job as a hotel assistant supervisor in what is now known as the Crowne Plaza, which is located on State Street in downtown Rochester, New York. He also worked in clothing and in a shoe factory, in the mid-1970s. After that, he moved to Star Hill, Delaware, where he was employed at a poultry factory and suffered back injury and as a result. It forced him into early retirement. Mr. Nicolas King's early retirement gave him a chance to work full time in civil rights.

In 1978, he met and married his wife in Delaware, they eventually moved to Rochester, a town that he had come to know and love, and in many ways, he felt what I had felt when I first came to Rochester, which was simply freedom. It was the place where they were raising their family. All the while, Mr. Nicolas King remained committed to social change, and in the late 1980s, he moved to Florida and gained prominence as a civil rights leader heading the SCLC chapter in Fort Walton Beach for the period of twelve years. And the fact that he did a superb job was as if it was what he was born to do. In 1997, Mr. Nicolas King received the Malcolm X Drum Major Award. Mr. King retired from Fort Walton and moved back to the city that he had come to know and love, but seeing some racist activities take place, Mr. Nicolas King came out of retirement and joined up with Reverend Jacob Cobs and founded the Monroe County Chapter SCLC in which time I would meet him. And because we trusted each other and could tell each other any and everything, one day Mr. King told me that he had undergone an operation for prostate cancer five years before he had met me, and that he had to take some kind of hormone shots every so often in order to keep the cancer from coming back. So we were going back and forth to the Strong Hospital for him to get those shots that he needed to keep the cancer from coming back. He was telling me that when he would take those shots in the past that he would feel good for a long time afterward, but now the shots that the nurse at Strong was giving him wasn't doing anything for him. So he thought that she wasn't really giving him his real medicine and that the nurse was lying to him about what she was shooting him up with, so he thought that she was using a placebo.

One day about a week after Mr. Nicolas King had gotten his shots I came downstairs and found him crying. Naturally, I asked him what was wrong. And he said that he was hurting in the lower part of his back and then he asked me if I had anything for pain. I gave him what I had around the house for pain, but as soon as it would wear off, he would be hurting again. We weren't doing much about the case, but in some cases, we were waiting on some of them to respond back, and I noticed that over the next two to three months, Mr. King was taking a lot of pain pills. Sometimes he would ask me to put some back rub over the spot that was hurting him so bad. He was sick and yet he was still trying to get things done. He organized and cohosted the first annual Monroe County Chapter SCLC banquet in Rochester at which he presented some major awards to both blacks and whites, who had at one time or another took a stand for social change. I witnessed some of them cry as their names were called, and they received their award because they thought that nobody had noticed, remembered, or even cared that they had taken a stand for justice.

Activist and comedian, Wyatt Fisher, was the guest speaker that night with Mr. Nicolas King being the cohost, and as he would take to the podium, I could see the pain in his face that he was hurting bad. He was in great pain, and every time that he would try to talk, he would have to cough. It hurt me to see my friend in so much pain. He was like a father to me and had brought so much hope to me and my family. Right then, all I was able to do was to go in the men's restroom and pray for him, and so I did. After the banquet, I finally talked him into going to the hospital to see what was causing him so much pain and why that he was taking so many pain pills. He had said that it may have been a disk in his back, but now that I think about it, I believed that he already knew what it was or he had an idea and didn't want the doctor to confirm it. I remember the day I drove him and his wife to the hospital. I pulled up and let them out at the door. I had to find a parking space so that made me the last person to come in. When I got in, I found out where they were and instantly I heard Mr. King saying, "Oh no! Oh no!" I heard his wife crying. I was confused because I didn't know what was going on. The doctor took me out in the hallway and told me that Mr. King only had two to four months to live. The cancer had come back and had spread to different parts of his body. They started his treatment, but he was slipping away fast. I could almost see the cancer eating him away because he was hospitalized, and I would go and see him every day after I got off work. It looked like he was losing weight daily. Sometimes I would sing church songs to him, and in others times, I would read the Bible to him and pray. My father had died from lung cancer just two years earlier and now it was my friend. Mr. King never got to meet my mother.

On Friday, March 24, I went to the hospital to check on him, and it was at that time that I told him that I loved him and that it hurt me to see him in so much pain. I also thanked him for all of his help. I told him that I was going to travel to Arkansas for a few days to take some pictures for my book, yes that's right, I was thinking about writing this book way back then, which is one of the reasons why I said at the start,

"If I had a dollar for every time that I thought about writing this book, I could have retired by now." I told Mr. King that I would see him as soon as I got back, and I would always end my visit with a prayer although by this time the cancer had progressed to the point that he could not talk. But this time, as I started to pray and ask God to spare his life, he waved his hand and stopped me as if he was saying that he was ready to go on and be with the Lord. I went on to Arkansas, and I was telling my mother all about how he was looking forward to coming to Arkansas to meet the family and how sick he was. My mom would tell me about how much she regretted not meeting him. On Thursday, March 30, 2000, I got the phone call that Mr. King had died. So again I found myself by myself in the fight for justice. And just like that my friend was gone and the case that was moving along so well had come to a standstill. I knew that I didn't have nowhere near the knowledge about the laws of civil rights as Mr. King had, but one thing that I was sure about and that was that I could not give up. I knew that Mr. King wouldn't have wanted me to. Although my mother never got to meet him, she came to New York the following summer after his death to visit, and when my mother got to my house and came in, she stopped in the middle of my living room floor and was looking around and then strangely she pointed to a chair that was at my dining room table and asked me if that was where Mr. King used to sit at when he would be talking to her on the phone? And I answered her yes. Then I asked her how did she know? Then she simply said that she could feel his presence. After much prayer, faith, and hope, I would continue to write letters and make contact with anybody that I thought would help us get an investigation, and in 2002, I contacted the Cochran Firm and on June 17, 2002, I received a letter from them saying that after an initial investigation, they decided not to accept my case. They said that their decision was not a reflection of the merits of my claim, but rather they were limited to the number of cases that they could accept. Therefore, they were sending me back the documents that I had provided their office. It was the same as others down through the years, "We can't help you, but we wish you success as you endeavor to vindicate your rights." On June 12, 2003, a letter was written to Danielle Berry, who at that time, a senator was telling her all about the tragedy that had taken place in Augusta, Woodruff County, Arkansas. I thought that because she was from Arkansas and at the time a senator in the great state of New York, which was where I was now living and the fact that I was from Arkansas, I could count on her to do all that was in her power to help aid me get an investigation, but to my surprise, I never even got a response. Meanwhile in between time, the good old boys of Woodruff County were still doing business as usual, around 2009, some of the black residents of Woodruff County witnessed when two white police officers arrested and picked up Mr. Timothy Williams; only it wasn't until later that it was revealed that he really wasn't arrested at all. And it just so happen that one of the policemen was Billy Earl, the same white guy who had hit me in the head years earlier, and he also was the same guy who had hung and killed Emma Lakes in the Woodruff County Jail. The other policeman who was with him was known as racist also. Mr. Timothy Williams was never seen again alive. After been missing for a few days, his dead body along with his bicycle was found in the White River as well. So for as it would be, Mr. Williams's death is just another black man who has been murdered at the hands of some white race-haters. There has been no investigation and no one has as much as spent a night in Woodruff County Jail for it. The blacks of Woodruff County talked about Mr. Williams's death, but only among themselves because they are afraid since nothing for all of these years has ever been done about the deaths of all the blacks that have been murdered at the hands of white race- haters, and that nothing is going to ever change. But by the grace of God, I am going to prove them wrong, because beside the many reason that I write this book, one of them is that it might lead the authorities to investigate the things that I am saying in this book. On August 5, 2013, I traveled to Woodruff County to meet with my oldest brother. On August 7, 2013, he and I went to Little Rock, Arkansas, to the field office of the Federal Bureau of Investigation to have a sit-down with them, and when we first arrived, we had to wait at the front gate to be cleared, then two of the duty agents came out and escorted us into the building and into a room. Although it was two of them, only one of them was asking us questions. He started out by asking what was the reason we had come to them. Since I was the one with the records and documents, I thought that it would only make sense that I would be the one to try and explain why we were there and what had happened. I started to talk, but every time that I would try to say something, he would cut me off with something negative, and the truth been told I had started thinking, *Here we go with some more race-hating people.* Finally I said, "Why do I feel like we're butting heads here?" Then the duty agent told me the reasons that it was the whos and the whys and if I was able to tell them the story. And as I was telling them the story, I was passing them documents to support my story and all that I was telling them. Eventually they looked at each other and then they asked to be excused, then the both of them got up and went out of the room. My brother and I looked at each other wondering what had just happened. Then they came back in the room, and the same one that was doing all of the talking started to explain that a part of their job was to see if our case was a Federal Bureau of Investigation matter and it was. Then he asked me if my mother was still alive. I answered him yes, and I told him that she was still hanging on.

Then the duty agent said to me, "I'm impressed with you, Kent, but I was busy putting all of the documents back in the carrying case."

I said, "I'm sorry I didn't hear you."

Then he said it again, "I'm impressed with you, Kent, because I'm holding a piece of paper in my hand that is dated 1992, and this happened back in 1984. I'm impressed with you." Then he said, "I don't need to see any more of those papers because it's only going to make me mad," then he said that he was so sorry for our loss, and that we could not have come to a better place. He finished the meeting with these words, "I only have one question, Kent, you seem to be bright and intelligent, what took you so long to come to us?" I didn't want to tell him that when we first moved to Newport that some men from the Bureau out of the Jonesboro office had come and talked to my mother and made little of the fact that we were saying that the kids were dead as a result of some white race-haters, and we never heard from them again. I thought that if I would have told him that he might said, "Oh, if the Bureau had already looked at this then we can't do anything." So I just let him think that it took me all of those years to come to the

Bureau. Then they asked for our contact information, and they wanted me to leave them the documents, but I told them that since I have had them all these years that I might as well keep them but that I would give them some copies, but that I was going to need a few days to get back to New York. A few days later, I was still in Arkansas, and I pulled up in my mother's yard to go in and say my good-byes because I was getting ready to leave back to New York, and my phone rung, it was the duty agent asking me how was I coming alone with those copies. I let him know that I was leaving Arkansas as he speaks. So it turned out that the duty agent that I had originally thought was a racist actually gave me my first real gleam of hope since Mr. King had died. When I got back to New York, I got the records and the documents that they wanted me to put together and sent them to them.

Meanwhile, my family and I are patiently waiting to hear their findings and reports. I firmly hope that our search for justice is over and that the authorities will find the truth and know what we have been living with for thirty long years. Now on March 2, 2014, made it to be thirty years since my family was murdered. Nevertheless, I am prepared to continue to search for justice, and I have not gave up yet, neither do I plan to until justice come forth or until I die, whichever one comes first. I not only wrote this book in efforts of getting an investigation for my family only, but for the families and loved ones of all of those who have lost their lives in Woodruff County to a wrongful death by racial injustice.

Also, I wrote this book for the sake of history that if this tragedy is ever visited in the future that they might know what the truth is and that is that we didn't kill our own family with an illegal gas hook up or a leak in a gas line but that our family was murdered by some white race-haters. I wrote this book also to show and tell America and the rest of the world about our struggle for justice. I know what the Apostle Paul meant (2 Cor. 4:8) when he said that "I have been troubled on every side yet not distressed. I've been perplexed but not in despair. I have been persecuted but not forsaken. I have been cast down but not destroyed," and thanks to God, I don't look like what I have been through and I still got my smile and every now and then, I catch myself laughing out loud. There was a time in my life growing up in Woodruff County that

I wished I was white because they had everything and we had nothing, but thanks to Mr. James Brown, I can truly say that I wouldn't want to be anybody else other than who I am and it all has brought me to a place in life where I am able to say that I am a man that can take a stand in the soil and the sand of America and say it loud from the bottom of my heart, "I am black and I am proud."

As I end this chapter, I would like to take this time to thank the families and loved ones of all those who have helped us down through the years in our struggle for justice, especially those who are no longer with us. Also my heart and prayers goes out to every family across this nation who has lost a loved one to the senseless killing of black-on-black crime in 2011. Out of all the violence that was committed in the United States 38.3 percent was blacks. Also in 2011, out of all of the arrests that were made in the United States 49.7 percent was blacks. It is my personal desire that this book serve as a reminder of our struggle as a people of color for civil rights and justice in this nation. For if this book would cause just one black man woman or child to put down their gun and not kill another then my writing would not have been in vain.

This is the station where the Fire Department secretary worked, and where momma stopped at on her way home. This also where they purchased the gas.

This is Woodruf County Jail, where I spent 28 of a 30 day sentence; also, where they hung Emma Lakes.

This is the fre station where the Paterson Police
parked their cars while they went to momma's
house to kill the kids.

This is the red snub nose fre truck that was
actually there that night.

This is the Wooddruf County Courthouse where
the Klu Klux Klan marched to, and held their
recruitment meeting.

This the fnal resting place of the murdered
kids, Buckeye Cemetary.

The white only cafe which blacks had to go through
the back door. It would eventually go private and
no blacks would be allowed at all.

Burned House (Front)

This is the front of the house that was fre bombed.

This is the side of the house where all of the kids
bodies where found, except for one.

Brian Before

Brian After

Curtis before

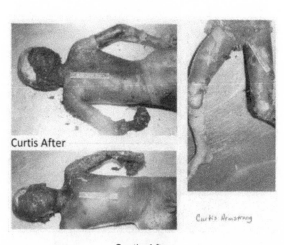

Curtis After

Ryan before

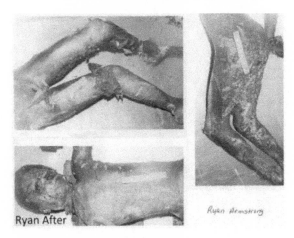

Ryan After

Tracy before

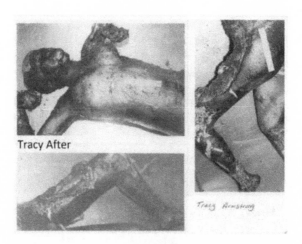

Tracy after

Otis before

Otis After

Leak in Gas Pipe Blamed For Augusta House Fire That Killed Five Children

Gazette State News

State Fire Marshal Ray Carnahan said Monday that a fire that killed five children Friday night in Augusta began from a leak in a flexible pipe leading to a small gas heater.

He said that the gas service to the house had been disconnected, but that apparently someone hooked it up again using a washing machine drain hose.

Brian Lee White Armstrong, 7, Curtis Elwood Armstrong, 8, Ryan Christian Armstrong, 11, Tracy Michelle Armstrong, 13, and Otis Valentine, 16, died in the fire. The Armstrong children were the children of Paula Armstrong. Otis Valentine was a cousin who was visiting.

Although the gas, electricity and water at the house had been turned off some time in February by Augusta's city-owned utility company for nonpayment of bills, Carnahan said that "the burn patterns around the heater and gas pipe indicated that gas was flowing through the pipe when the fire started."

Carnahan said the utility company had taken away the gas meter at the house, leaving only a gas pipe at the side of the house. The pipe was closed with a valve, he said. Apparently, Carnahan said, someone had opened the valve and connected the pipe to the house's gas system with a flexible hose normally used as a drain for a washing machine.

"When I got there," Carnahan said, "the hose was not on the pipe. It was laying on the ground near the pipe, but the indications of the burn patterns were that there was some gas flowing into the house."

He said the hose appeared to have been tied to the pipe with a shoestring.

No Part in Fire

Despite the flimsy nature of the outside gas hookup, Carnahan said, it apparently played no part in the actual starting of the fire. His investigation of the burned-out one-story frame house indicated that the fire was caused by a leak in a flexible metal gas line from the heater to the living room gas pipe, he said.

"The fire began in the living room in and around a small gas space heater that was placed near to an overstuffed chair," he said.

Carnahan said there were two other heaters in the house, both of them fueled by wood. The children were found in a back bedroom, he said.

"There were no smoke detectors in the house," he said. "By the time the fire in the living room was discovered, it was out of control, and there was no escape route for those kids. They couldn't get to either the front door or the back door without going through the flames. There's no doubt in my mind that a smoke detector could have saved those children."

COOL HORN — Al Porter Jr., an Arkansas native who now lives in Chicago, opened the August in Arkansas festival at Little Rock's Riverfront Park Thursday night. *Review, 5B; more on festival in the Weekend section.*

Malak seeks examiner job

Arkansas record reportedly gives Guam concern

BY JERRY DEAN
Democrat-Gazette Staff Writer

Dr. Fahmy Malak, Arkansas' controversial former state medical examiner, has sought a similar $160,000-a-year job as chief medical examiner in Guam, a U.S. Trust Territory island in the southern Marianas.

But Malak's chances of landing the new job may have paled last week because of apparent inconsistencies in a resume he presented to job interviewers on the 209-square-mile island.

Elizabeth Barrett-Anderson, Guam's attorney general who also heads the territory's Post-mortem Examination Commission, which is seeking a new medical examiner, said in an article published last week in the

But Malak's chances of landing the new job may have paled last week because of apparent inconsistencies in a resume.

Pacific Daily News that Malak applied for the job last December and was interviewed in June.

Malak's resume also stated he had held an assistant professor's post at the University of Arkansas for Medical Sciences while serving 12 years as the state medical examiner. When questioned later about the re-

sume item, Malak said he actually had been a lower-ranking assistant professor.

Further checks by Dr. Hee Vong Park, Guam's retiring medical examiner, revealed Malak had been an unpaid clinical assistant professor at UAMS in Little Rock.

Upon Malak's resignation Sept. 10, 1991, from the Arkansas medical examiner's post, he began working for the state Health Department as a consultant and was paid $70,000 a year.

Shannon Murphy, a reporter at the *News*, said Thursday that the question of Malak's employment had been deferred at least until Monday so Malak could respond to the panel's concerns about his Arkansas tenure.

Conway annexation efforts impede plans to provide water, fire service to area

vanced to the AA State Tournament, by defeating Lobiais, Saturday night.
They are, kneeling, left to right, Lisa Freeman, Sonya Mauldin, Jennifer Mc-
Donald, Chantel Ayers, and Debra Vann. Standing, left to right, Gale Norwood,
Bobbi Taylor, Lori Simmons, Lisa Holiday, Wendy Davis, Beth Hopkins, Chris
McDonald, and Tori Buchanan.

Five Augusta children die in house fire early Friday; gas leak blamed for blaze

Five Augusta children, ranging in age from seven to 16 years, died in a house fire early Friday morning.

State Fire Marshal Ray Carnahan investigated the fire and ruled out the possibility of arson as the cause of the blaze.

Sheriff Leon Creasey stated that the blaze definitely was the result of an illegal gas tap. He said that utilities had been cut off from the house because of non-payment. The sheriff added that on two previous occasions an illegal gas tap had been discovered at the residence.

The victims were Tracy Michele Armstrong, 11; Ryan Christian Armstrong, 13; Curtis Elwood Armstrong, 8; Bryan Lee White Armstrong, 7, and a cousin, Odis Valentine, 16.

The bodies of all the children were sent to the state medical examiner to determine the cause of death.

Chief Palmer of the state medical examiner's office notified Sheriff Creasey Monday morning that all five of the children died as the result of smoke inhalation. He said the autopsy report showed a 70 to 76 per cent carbon monoxide in their blood streams.

Sheriff Creasey said neighbors reported hearing two explosions and finding the one-story frame home engulfed in flames. The fire was reported at 12:45 Friday morning and by the time firemen arrived, the roof of the house had collapsed.

Capt. Carl Banner of the Augusta Police Department said the explosions heard by neighbors were probably the sounds of exploding aerosol cans and a television picture tube reacting to the intense heat of the fire.

According to Sheriff Creasey the children were apparently in the house alone when the fire broke out. "We don't know if they tried to get out," he said. "One of them had on a pair of sneakers. The fire may have gotten between them and the door." The bodies of two of the children were

healer.

His report continued:
The gas service to the house had been disconnected, but that apparently someone hooked it up again using a washing machine drain hose.

Although the gas, electricity and water at the house had been turned off some time in February by Augusta's city-owned utility company for non-payment of bills, "the burn patterns around the heater and gas pipe indicated that gas was flowing through the pipe when the fire started."

The utility company had taken away the gas meter at the house, leaving only a gas pipe at the side of the house. The pipe was closed with a valve," he said. Apparently someone had opened the valve and connected the pipe to the home's gas system with a flexible hose normally used as a drain for a washing machine.

"When I got there," Carnahan said, "the hose was out on the pipe. It was laying on the ground near the pipe, but the indications of the burn patterns were that there was some gas flowing into the house."

He said the hose appeared to have been tied to the pipe with a shoestring.

Despite the flimsy nature of the outside gas hookup, Carnahan said, it apparently played no part in the actual starting of the fire. His investigation of the burned-out one-story frame house indicated that the fire was caused by a leak in a flexible metal line from the heater in the living room gas pipe.

"The fire began in the living room in and around a small gas space heater that was placed near to an overstuffed chair," he said.

Carnahan said there were two other heaters in the house, both of them fueled by wood. The children were found in a back bedroom, he said.

"There were no smoke detectors in the house," he said.

Cotton Plant man dies in fire

Leonard George, 28, of

Duane Fraser to be honored at luncheon

An awards luncheon honoring Duane Fraser of the Patton Chapel community as the state winner in a corn yield contest will be held Friday noon at Ferrell's Restaurant.

Fraser was judged the winner of a National Corn Growers Assn. contest with a yield of 182.24 bushels per acre. The championship yield was from RA102 seed, a product of King Around Seed Co. of Dallas, and was planted on irrigated land.

The Woodruff County farmer planted about 300 acres in corn of three varieties, all from the Ring Around company. Lawhon Farm Supply of McCrory is the local retail dealer for the seed and J. R. McGill is the area representative.

Gary Hawkins new McCrory Police Chief

Gary Hawkins, an experienced law enforcement officer and private investigator, has been employed as Chief of Police in the City of McCrory. He assumed his duties on March 1.

Chief Hawkins is a native of Oklahoma, the son of Donald and Ona Hawkins, who now live in Salesville, Ark. His wife, the former Carolyn Brooks, is a native of Valley View, near Jonesboro, and they are parents of a daughter, Natalie.

After graduation from Enid, Okla., High School, Hawkins attended the University of Hawaii, the University of North Carolina, the University of Arkansas at Fayetteville and Arkansas State University, Jonesboro, where he majored in law enforcement and criminology. At the National Open University in Washington, D. C., he studied investigation and security.

He spent 11 years in the Marine Corps where he was a staff sergeant and intelligence chief. He has served as patrolman in the Mountain Home Police Department and was a captain and uniform commander in the

Freeman with 16 points. Simmons led the rebounding charts with 12, while the rest of the team combined for 18 rebounds, 12 steals and one blocked shot.

On Saturday the girls advanced to the finals against a tough Gosnell team. The first quarter was the key period as the Lady Jags outscored Gosnell 14-6. In the second quarter the Lady Pirates hung tough as the scoring slacked off for both teams, but the Jags went in at half with a seven point lead after a last second shot by Tori Buchanan. In the third quarter the Pirates outscored the Lady Jags 8-6 and in the fourth put up a tough defensive effort and outscored the Jaguars 11-4, which tied the ballgame at 34-34 on a three point play at the buzzer. In the first overtime the Pirates held the ball for a last second attempt which failed. The second overtime was controlled by the McCrory girls but an attempt at the last second shot was also unsuccessful.

The third overtime was one of several opportunities for both teams to score but lay-ups were missed by Gosnell and turnovers plagued the Jags with both teams missing free throws. With one minute left, the Jags decided to go for broke and put some added pressure on the ball and caused the Pirates to make a bad pass. Lisa Freeman was there to pick up the ball and go down for the uncontested lay-up to go ahead 36-34. Last second efforts made by Gosnell to score were unsuccessful and the girls finally heard the buzzer go off for the last time.

Wendy Davis, Lisa Holiday, Lisa Freeman were named to the All Tournament Team. Davis was selected as the tournament's Most Valuable Player.

Home Box Office now available on McCrory TV

Paul Eddington, owner of the McCrory Cable Television, this week announced that Home Box Office is now available in this area to those customers who are already subscribers of Showtime. Eddington stated that HBO will be added permanently to this system and customers may subscribe to either or both of the optional services. Interested persons who call the Cable TV office before

McCrory Leader.

No purchase is necessary to register in every store that is a Shopper's Dream promotion.

Merchants participating in Store. Bur-Mack's Department, McCrory, Byrd Glass and Paint, Hardware and Sporting Goods Supply, The Friendly Store, Jr. and Radiator Repair of Patton, Flower and Gift Shop, Farm Shelter Insurance Co., Crossroads Country, M&M Water Conditioning Service, S & H Pharmacy, Buick of Augusta, Art's Electronics (two weeks) and Thermogas of Augusta (five weeks).

The first advertisements in Leader next week and the first March 23 at 1:30 p.m.

County Democrats Saturday to state convention of presidential candidate

Democrats in the nine Woodruff County justice of peace districts will decide the 1984 presidential preference of the Woodruff County Democratic Party in caucuses throughout the county Saturday morning. Democrats who visit the caucuses will have the choice of the four presidential candidates who have qualified on a state-wide basis in Arkansas, or they may cast their vote as uncommitted.

The presidential candidates who have qualified in Arkansas are John Glenn, Gary Hart, Jesse Jackson and Walter Mondale.

Justice of Peace districts one, two and three, with their chairpersons, Kino Reeves, Duane Fraser and Cleo Cain, will meet at the McCrory City Hall.

Districts four and five, with chairpersons Roy Bengel and Roy Robinson, will meet at the Cotton Plant City Hall.

District six, with chairperson, Hoyle Lindsey, will meet at the Gregory Community Center.

The Woodruff County northeast will be the site of meetings of districts seven, eight and nine, with chairpersons Inez Neiderer, Marsha Wilson and Noel Madison. All meetings are slated to begin promptly at ten a.m. and once the meeting has been called to order, no other persons will be admitted to the room.

Arkansas Democrats this

Arkansas

2 change Malak rulings on 4 deaths, sustain 10

HONORED TEACHER — Lt. Gov. Jim Guy Tucker honors Annemary Favorite.

State picks its teacher

of the year

FBI to investigate 34 ballots in race

6B • THURSDAY, FEBRUARY 5, 1998 • • A

Police 'maliciously' slew man

BY LINDA FRIEDLIEB
ARKANSAS DEMOCRAT-GAZETTE.

Law enforcement officers in Jackson and Woodruff counties killed, then castrated a man before finally hiding his body, the Newport men's family alleges in a lawsuit filed Friday in federal court in Little Rock.

But a news account at the time and some law enforcement authorities on Monday said Bryant L. Brown, 26, shot himself April 23, 1997, after shooting a former girlfriend he had kidnapped.

Woodruff County Sheriff Jack

Caperton said the castration was done at the state Crime Laboratory, where experts were checking to see if Brown had been bruised.

Brown was riding in a car with his former girlfriend, Brandie N. Green, when he came upon a roadblock on Arkansas 33 in southern Jackson County, the lawsuit alleges. Officers shot Brown while he sat in the car, the suit says.

The suit, assigned to U.S. District Judge Henry Woods, targets the counties, naming as defendants their quorum courts and sheriffs; and the cities of McCrory

and Newport, naming their city councils and police officers. Additional officers, including some Arkansas State Police troopers, are also named as defendants, as is Green, who survived.

The lawsuit alleges that the officers violated several federal laws and the First, Fourth, Fifth, Eighth and 14th Amendments of the U.S. Constitution.

"The defendants took aim with their weapons, and without legal justification, willfully, maliciously and intentionally fired their weapons at [Brown], hiding him on the left side

Arkansas Democrat 🌟 Gazette

at roadblock, suit claims

of the head," the lawsuit says.

The lawsuit contends that Brown was then taken away by ambulance to an unknown place, where he was castrated and some body parts were removed without the family's permission.

Caperton, who said he was not present, said Brown was considered armed and dangerous and that a state trooper had been tailing the car. "The only shots fired at the scene were fired within the car," he said.

After the shooting, Caperton said, Brown was taken away by

ambulance but was pronounced dead before the ambulance could reach a hospital.

Stacy Barker, former McCrory police chief, gave a similar report Monday although he said he thought Brown was castrated to determine how long it had been since he had intercourse.

"But none of that happened that the family claimed," said Barker, not specifically named as a defendant.

David Stewart, Newport's police chief, declined to comment, saying only that he had not yet

been served with the lawsuit. Jackson County Sheriff Jim Bishop also declined to comment on pending litigation and said crime reports had been turned over to the Arkansas State Police, who handled the investigation.

Bill Sadler, a state police spokesman, said he could not comment on pending litigation. He also said he was having difficulty finding records of the event Monday afternoon.

Green does not have a listed number in the Newport telephone book.

136

5 Children Die in Augusta Fire; Arson Called Possibility

Gazette State News

AUGUSTA — Five children, ranging in age from 7 to 16, died in a house fire early Friday, and Woodruff County Sheriff Leon Creasey said officials "will definitely investigate the possibility of arson."

Creasey said neighbors reported hearing two explosions and finding the one-story frame home engulfed in fire. The fire was reported at 12:53 a.m. and by the time firemen arrived, the roof of the house had collapsed.

The bodies of Brian Lee White Armstrong, 7, Curtis Elwood Armstrong, 8, Ryan Christian Armstrong, 11, Tracy Michelle Armstrong, 13, and Otis Valentine, 16, were all found in a bedroom, the sheriff said. All of the Armstrongs were the children of Paula Armstrong. Valentine was a cousin visiting the home.

'Looking Real Close'

The sheriff said officers had been called to the house recently because of "a little row" and because of that "we are looking at this fire real close." State Fire Marshal Ray Carnahan was investigating the fire in order to determine its cause, and

(See FIVE on Page 8A.)

State Fire Marshal Ray Carnahan (left). Carl Bunner sift through remains of living room.

Texas pathologist rules 1987 death a homicide

BY DOUG THOMPSON
Democrat-Gazette Benton Bureau

The 1987 death of Randall Wayne Brady, 32, of Little Rock was "a plain case of homicide," Dr. Marc Krouse said Thursday during an ongoing evaluation of a dozen controversial cases from the state medical examiner's office.

Brady's death was ruled a suicide when it happened, a ruling which Dr. Fahmy Malak later changed to indicate an undetermined cause of death while still medical examiner. Malak, whose home telephone number is unlisted, could not be reached—for comment Thursday evening.

Brady was not shot by himself. There is no question about it," said Krouse, a deputy medical examiner in Tarrant County, Texas.

Krouse and Dr. Michael Graham, a professor at the St. Louis University School of Medicine, are reviewing 12 controversial cases for the state Crime Laboratory Board. The pathologists met July 9 and 10 with family members in the cases involved to give a progress report and interview them for further information.

In a related development, Krouse and Graham said in a tape-recorded interview with the family of Olivia "Janie" Ward, 16, of Searcy County that
See MALAK, Page 10A

Veterans of Persian Gulf War suffering mysterious illnesses

BY ED TIMMS
AND STEVE McGONIGLE

DALLAS — Gary Zuspann, a former Navy petty officer, has difficulty breathing and is so weak that he can barely walk to the back gate of his home in nearby Euless, Texas.

Marine Capt. David Fournel used to run three miles a day, lift workout with weights. Then he suffered congestive heart failure. He still endures

Army Sgt. Greg Wolf has urinary tract problems and sometimes is so tired that he can barely hold up his head. His muscles, he said, "are just Jell-O."

They are among dozens of Persian Gulf War veterans who are suffering from illnesses that have defied diagnosis.

Many complain of chronic fatigue, depression and pain in their joints or muscles. Some

BY RACHEL O'NEAL
Democrat-Gazette Capitol Bureau

The state may not have enough legislators to conduct a legislative session in January if the recently approved term-limit amendment is retroactive, officials warned Friday.

Voters approved Tuesday an amendment that limits the terms of state and federal officeholders. Many legislators have questioned aspects of the amendment.

"There is a school of thought that we may have to adjourn the legislative session and go home until this is finally resolved," Sen. Allen Gordon of Morrilton said Friday.

"We could meet down there in January and ultimately [a court's] interpretation could invalidate any action taken by legislators affected by the amendment," Gordon added.

Opponents of the term-limit amendment have predicted the

issue will wind up in court.

But Gordon said a lawsuit challenging the amendment probably wouldn't be filed by the Legislature.

"There is a real reluctance among the Legislature to firing any type of action that would directly attack an action by the people who wanted it passed," Gordon said.

Members of Term Limits Now — the group that sponsored the amendment — said in a statement released Friday that politicians are looking for ways to "thwart" the amendment.

The amendment limits state representatives to three two-year terms and state senators to two four-year terms.

If the amendment applies retroactively, only 12 of the Senate's 35 members would be eligible to serve. And only 32 of the House's 100 members would be eligible. Both figures include 22 new legislators who were elect-

ed this year. The total in one or two-year-posed newly elected representative Vada Sheid of Mountain Home, who has already served five terms in the House.

In June, House Speaker Rep. John Lipton of Warren-Bradley County asked for an attorney general's opinion on several questions, whether the amendment would apply retroactively; whether a House member who served the maximum number of years would be eligible to run as a Senate candidate; and whether the amendment includes nonconsecutive terms.

In the opinion, Attorney General Winston Bryant found that his staff could not address the question until the amendment had been approved by voters.

Lawrence Graves, the attorney general's chief of staff, said that as of Friday no other request for an opinion had been made.

Rulings

● Continued from Page 1B

Crime Laboratory, disagreed, saying autopsies are highly dependent on evidence collected by criminal investigators.

"Police investigation and criminal investigation in Arkansas ranges from very good to poor," Clark said. "To make the ruling of cause or manner of death, you have to depend heavily on the information that comes into the agency from the outside."

Gain said the changes in manner and cause of death in the four cases will be passed along to appropriate investigating agencies. The agencies will decide whether further investigation is warranted, she said.

The board voted to make the pathologists' reports public, subject to a review by the attorney general's office.

The 10 cases in which the independent pathologists agreed

with the original conclusion for cause and manner of death will remain open if further information comes to light, the board voted. Decisions could be changed by the pathologists in any of the 14 cases if new information is received.

The cases where the pathologists agreed with the original determinations were:

● The 1993 drowning death of Jimmy Seagrist of North Little Rock. Malak ruled the death as accidental. The family contends that a bullet in Seagrist's head was overlooked.

● The 1988 death of Larran C. Carlton of Cleveland County. Malak ruled that Carlton died accidentally by inhaling food. The family contends that Carlton was murdered.

● The 1986 shooting deaths of Gerald "Tiny" Jumper and his ex-wife, Clara Jumper of Palestine [St. Francis County]. Malak ruled that Gerald Jumper shot his ex-wife, then shot himself. The family suspects foul play.

● The 1986 shooting death of Dorothy House of Washington County. Malak ruled the death a suicide, but the family suspects foul play.

● The 1987 shooting death of Brenda Sue Stewart of Washington County. Malak ruled the death a suicide. The family suspects foul play.

● The 1988 shooting death of Ted Frier of White County. Malak ruled the death a suicide. The family believes he was murdered.

● The 1990 shooting death of William Webb of Pulaski County. Malak ruled the death a homicide. The family of Webb's wife, who allegedly shot her husband, questioned why the death was considered a homicide.

● The 1992 shooting death of Bill White of Hot Springs. Malak ruled the death a suicide. The family suspects foul play.

● The 1993 shooting death of Jerry McCool of East End [Saline County]. Malak ruled the death a suicide, but the family

thinks it was an accident or murder.

In other business, the board approved a motion aimed to reduce the workload at the medical examiner's office. State pathologists would rely more heavily on external examination or partial autopsies to save time.

"In a certain percentage of cases, we can determine cause of death by external examination and a review of patient records," said Assistant Medical Examiner Frank Peretti.

The new policy was not hailed by some of the people involved in the TV colloquium.

"I'm incensed," said Linda Ives of Bryant, founder of Victims of Malak's Incredible Testimony. Ives' son, Kevin, and another Bryant youth, Don Henry, were hit by a train in 1987. Malak concluded that the boys smoked marijuana and fell asleep on the tracks. A grand jury later ruled the deaths homicide.

GOP

● Continued from Page 1B

issue as people learn about the Republican philosophy and move away from the Yellow Dog Democrat thinking, he said.

"I think we'll all benefit from a two-party system," Cotton said.

Cotton said the party's goal for the next election will be to field a candidate for every major position.

The victories of Greg Wren, an independent for state representative, and Garrison and the crossover votes in other races "proves this county is willing to vote for somebody other than a Democrat," said Frank Arey, first vice chairman of the county Republican Party. Garrison's victory will help to reverse Republican

STATION KSR-930

STATION LOG

A.M.

DATE 3-2-84   DEPT. SO   OPERATOR _____

This paper shows that Patterson police was in town before the fire started.

TIME	CALLED	CALLED BY	INFORMATION ON CALL OR BROADCAST
12:00	938	Lois	10-8 3-2
12:01	611	Sonny	Patterson Police car out side of Fire Station around - ck car everything okay with the car, at Bill's car is inside, is not around
12:03	604	Spec	out of car a few
12:04	Pat	S. Lomas	Called again about her husband as it he may take her kids off with them
12:09	604	Spec	10-8
12:23	604	"	10-8
12:50	415	Jim	10-28 Ola
12:52	Pat	Service	Truck exploded
		Jim	Home Trailer on fire Family inside - Okay
		Jeff	Call 803-801
		Jim	Call 803-814
			to Bill Angelo Jim ton
		Forrest	
		Sheriff	
		Willie	call 10-8
		R Lohr	
		Angelo	
1:23	601	Sheriff	10-97
1:30	603	Carl	how Willie go get 2 i the bill & burn the

Fourteen other people were murdered,
this is the White River where three of those
bodies were found.

Note: This paper is the proof showing that the Askansas State Crime Lab was actively engaged in taking pictures of three additional bodies outside of my families total of five losses. According to the last entry of the spreadsheet, the body was consider an unknown person.

ARKANSAS STATE CRIME LAB PHOTO SECTION

RECEIPT FORM

I HAVE RECEIVED THIS DATE THE FOLLOWING ITEMS:

LOG #	MER #	QTY	ITEM DESCRIPTION			
12-409	84-84	5	Color negatives and 5 contact prints			
	85-84	5			5	
	86-84	4			4	
	87-84	2			2	
	88-84	4			4	
	89-84	17			17	
	90-84	6			6	
	91-84	12			12	
	Unk.	3			3	

SIGNATURE OF RECIPIENT: Pat Calhoun   DATE: 3/20/84

PRINTED NAME (IF NECESSARY): _____   SECTION: MEDX

Date 01-03-__   Page No. _____

STATEMENT OF: JIMMY L. MOORE, POLICE CHIEF, AUGUSTA POLICE DEPT.

AT 12:53 A.M. THIS DATE I RECEIVED A CALL FROM THE WOODRUFF COUNTY S.O.
RADIO DISPATCHER THAT SHE HAD RECEIVED A CALL THAT A HOUSE HAD "BLOWN UP"
ON SOUTH FIFTH ST. IN AUGUSTA. I ARRIVED AT THE SCENE ABOUT TWO (2) MINUTES
LATER AND FOUND A HOUSE LOCATED ON SOUTH FIFTH, COMPLETELY ENGULFED IN FLA
THERE WAS LOUD POPPING NOISES COMING FROM THE HOUSE THAT SOUNDED LIKE SHOT-
GUN SHELLS EXPLODING. THE FIRE DEPT. ARRIVED ABOUT ONE MINUTE AFTER I DID. .
AFTER THE FIRE WAS CONTAINED, FIVE (5) BODIES WERE REMOVED FROM A ROOM ON
THE SOUTHWEST CORNER OF THE HOUSE. THE BODIES WERE REMOVED BY WOODRUFF CO.
CORONOR, BILL ANGELO AND JIM RHODES. BODIES WERE IDENTIFIED AS FOLLOWS

BRYAN LEE WHITE ARMSTRONG	B/M DOB 02-11-77	AGE 7
CURTIS ELWOOD ARMSTRONG	B/M DOB 05-05-75	AGE 8
RYAN CHRISTIAN ARMSTRONG	B/M DOB 02-17-73	AGE 11
TRACIE MICHELLE ARMSTRONG	B/F DOB 01-17-73	AGE 13
OTIS VALENTINE B&E V-1	B/M DOB 02-15-68	AGE 16

FIRE SCENE IS BEING INVESTIGATED BY THE ARKANSAS STATE POLICE FIRE MARSHALL.
INVESTIGATION TO CONTINUE

**Note: This paper outlines the activity of
an explosion at the house. The Chief of
Police admitted the fact of an explosion
at the scene. Also, in a hand written
entry he made note of the possibility of
another unknown body.**

CRIMINAL INVESTIGATION DIVISION

TYPED
UNDEXED
LOGGED
PROOFED
QUAL. CON.
COPIED
FILED

ASP-3-A

DATE: April 3, 1984
DICTATED BY: LIEUTENANT CARNAHAN
DATE TYPED: April 6, 1984
COPIES TO: Police Chief Jim Moore, Augusta P.D.
                              Dr. Fahmy Malak, State Crime Lab

ADDENDUM TO CRIME SCENE SEARCH

On Wednesday, March 28, 1984 at 12:30 p.m, this investigator accompanied
by Mr. MYRON E. THOMPSON, Pipeline Safety Engineer of the Arkansas
Public Service Commission and Mr. ROBERT E. HENRY, Engineer Technician
of the Arkansas Public Service Commission examined the gas service
piping at 505 South 5th Street, Augusta, Arkansas. The gas riser
meter spud was examined and was found to have an inside dimension of
7/8 inside the dimension and d one inch outside diameter dimension.
The meter spud on the west side still had the packing in tact.

The 15 inch long black rubber hose which was found underneath the gas
piping at this location on the search of March 2, 1984 was compared to
the gas metal pipes and it was found that the black rubber hose would
not fit up onto the meter spud and that the way in which the black
rubber hose was cut would not allow for a fit snug enough around the
metal piping.

The area around the house was examined for any evidence of other
hoses or material that could have been used to circumvent the missing
gas meter, and none was found.

FILE NUMBER: 36-564-84   CRIME: Fire Investigation

**Note: This paper contains the finding of the Public
Service Commision, which proves that their was no
illegal gas hook-up and there was no leakage in any
of the gas lines at the house.**

9 781643 146089